FROM

OSWIECIM

TO

AUSCHWITZ: POLAND REVISITED

FROM
OSWIECIM
TO
AUSCHWITZ:
POLAND REVISITED

by Moshe Weiss

Mosaic Press
Oakville-Buffalo-London

Canadian Cataloguing in Publication Data

Weiss, Moshe, 1919-
    From Oswiecim to Auschwitz

ISBN 0-88962-558-1 (bound) ISBN 0-88962-557-3 (pbk.)

1. Weiss, Moshe, 1919-
2. Poland - Description and travel - 1981 -
3. Jews - Poland - History. I. Title.

DK4081.W45 1994   914.3804'56   C94-931025-5

Published by MOSAIC PRESS, P.O. Box 1032, Oakville, Ontario, L6J 5E9, Canada. Offices and warehouse at 1252 Speers Road, Units #1&2, Oakville, Ontario, L6L 5N9, Canada and Mosaic Press, 85 River Rock Drive, Suite 202, Buffalo, N.Y., 14207, USA.

Mosaic Press acknowledges the assistance of the Canada Council, the Ontario Arts Council, the Ontario Ministry of Culture, Tourism and Recreation and the Dept. of Communications, Government of Canada, for their support of our publishing programme.

Cover by Patty Gallinger
Typeset by Jackie Ernst
Printed and bound in Canada
ISBN 0-88962-558-1 (bound)
ISBN 0-88962-557-3 (pbk.)

In Canada:
    MOSAIC PRESS, 1252 Speers Road, Units #1&2, Oakville, Ontario, L6L 5N9, Canada. P.O. Box 1032, Oakville, Ontario, L6J 5E9
In the United States:
    Mosaic Press, 85 River Rock Drive, Suite 202, Buffalo, N.Y., 14207
In the U.K.
    John Calder (Publishers) Ltd., 9-15 Neal Street, London, WC2 H9TU, England

TABLE OF CONTENTS

FOREWORD

I am grateful to God for giving me the strength to write down what my eyes have seen, and what my ears have heard, and what my heart has felt during the many weeks and months that I have spent traveling through the length and breadth of the cities, towns, and villages of Poland to seek out the almost non-existent remains of Jewish life.

During my travels, I visited hundreds of once flourishing and now destroyed Jewish communities. Some of the Jews that I visited live alone in distant and forsaken places. When, after long conversations, I presented a small gift of a *siddur* or a *mezuzah* or a *talit*, the emotion was intense. "I have not held a *siddur* in my hands since 1939," one survivor told me. Another old man fell upon my shoulders when I draped a *talit* on his back and recited the blessing with him. "My back has not been warmed by a prayer shawl for over fifty years," he cried. I was the first Jew who had visited him in nearly half a century. He considered himself to be a forgotten Jew.

Even to this day, the post-war generation still does not recognize or appreciate what Polish Jewry represented. Their daily struggle for existence was merely the physical covering beneath which flourished a spiritual life of awesome richness and depth. For a thousand years, the Jews of Poland created a world embellished by learning, good deeds, redemption and spirituality. Then, in less than a decade, all of this was destroyed, disappearing into the smokestacks of the crematoria of Auschwitz and other killing centers, vanishing almost as if it had never existed.

But it had existed. And it was in quest of this world that once was that I journeyed again and again back to Poland, and what struck me over and over was the almost incomprehensible enormity of our loss. Wherever my feet brought me, to whichever mountain of devastation I arrived, I was reminded of the catastrophe. Everywhere, the cry, ''Remember me, Remember me,'' seemed to be rising up in lush green fields that appeared so innocent but where, not so long ago, atrocities and suffering of an indescribable magnitude had taken place. My sisters Chaya Yehudit and Adele, and my brother Yechezkel Shraga and their entire families--all of them seemed to be calling out to me and I could not rest.

For me, the spiritual satisfaction of visiting the pitiful remnants of our people in Poland, of bringing them news of the vibrant Jewish life beyond their borders, was immense. It was, in effect, as close as I could come to my brothers and sisters. It was a pilgrimage that I was privileged to undertake, and it is in this pilgrimage that I now invite my readers to join me.

In bringing this manuscript to completion, I wish to acknowledge the help and encouragement of my family: my wife, Sara Seidman Weiss; my daughters, Sara Tov, and Tova Reich and her husband, Walter Reich; and my sons and their wives, Avraham and Toby Weiss, Mordechai and D'vorah Weiss, and David and Nora Weiss.

Thanks is also due to my friends and colleagues, the editors at *The Jewish Press*,Rabbi Sholem Klass in which this book first appeared in significantly different form in seventy installments over several years , and to Mrs. Sheila Abrams, for their friendship, suggestions, and guidance. Thankyou to the readers of the manuscript and for their helpful comments:
Mr. Elie Wiesel, Dr. Abner Weiss, Dr. David Lehrfild, Rabbi Elazar Muskin, Rabbi Simcha Friedman, Dr. Abe Speiser, Mr. Amnon Ajsenstadt, Rabbi Norman Lipson, the publishers and readers of the Mosaic Press, Dr. Howard Aster and his staff.

I wish, finally, to pay tribute to the memory of my late wife, Miriam Borenstein Weiss, who supported me with exemplary loyalty and love in this undertaking from the very beginning.

Chapter 1.
FROM OSWIECIM TO AUSCHWITZ

For most Jews, the name Auschwitz evokes images of unrelieved horror and dread, but for me, the sense of this place is perhaps even more complex and nuanced. For Auschwitz was the bucolic Polish town in which I passed my childhood, where I received my early Hebrew education from the *melamed*, Reb Lazar, and from Chazzan Wilchford, where I put on *tefilin* for the first time and delivered my bar mitzvah *pilpul* at the long table in the Bobover *shtibel* on Ulica Berka Yoselowicza, also known as "Die Yiddishe Gass," the Jewish street.

Auschwitz, a name that has seared itself on the collective memory of humanity as the place of ultimate terror, is called by the Poles Oswiecim, but we Jews, who, in those days, constituted two-thirds of its population of 12,000, called it Oshpitzin, a word that means guests. Oshpitzin was home for us, and into our home we welcomed all guests and extended our hospitality to all travelers. For me, the transformation of Oshpitzin to Auschwitz signified the end of home and of innocence. When Oshpitzin/Oswiecim became Auschwitz, the bright sky of my childhood, and, indeed, the childhood of all mankind, was forever darkened by unthinkable evil.

Yet however blackened the place has become for me and for our people, it was necessary to return. One cannot escape one's childhood or one's history; a thousand years of Jewish history had played itself out in Poland after all. Irresistible forces drew me back again in search of my family and the remnants of my people. It was here that my grandfather, Reb Anschel, the son of Reb Mordechai "Sheloner," was orphaned as a young boy and taken into the household of the Sanzer Tzaddik, Rabbi Chaim Halberstam, author of *Divrei Chaim*. Along with the dozens of other young orphans reared by the Sanzer Tzaddik, my grandfather became known as one of the *Yaldei Sanz*. My father, Reb David, later joined the ranks of the *Shiniver Bachurim*, the disciples of Reb Chaim's son, Rabbi Yechezkel "Shiniver" Halberstam, author of *Divrei Yechezkel*. It was the Shiniver Rav himself who proposed the match between my father and Sarah, the daughter of his *gabbai*, Reb Anschel.

It was here in Poland that two of my sisters and my brother, as well as their entire families, were murdered: Chaya Yehudit and her husband, the *sofer*, Moshe Mayer Zigeltuch; Adele and her husband, Wolf Yaakov Datner; and my brother Yechezkel Shraga and his family. Refused permission to travel to the United States as part of our family, they wept inconsolably when we left, almost as if they had a premonition of the fate that awaited them.

And it is here to Poland that I came in quest of not only my family, but of the remains of my Jewish brothers and sisters. *Et achai anochi mevakesh*: I am seeking my brothers. These words were like a beacon to me as I traveled from city to city, town to town, village to village, seeking out the remnants of the approximately five thousand Jews, most of them aged and impoverished, all that is left of a once vibrant and flourishing population of nearly three and one half million.

My most recent missions to Poland took place in the spring of 1990, 1991, 1992 and 1993. After my first return visit over three decades ago, in 1959, I was able to coordinate the shipment of packages of clothing and goods to the survivors of our people in Poland and to bring their greetings to the American community. Those of us who come from that world carry it constantly within our hearts and our memories. However blackened that memory has become, however heartsick we feel when we recall what has taken place, I have discovered that men and women still long for news of their brothers and sisters, and they yearn, too, for word of the world they left behind.

Chapter 2.
WARSAW

During my first return visit to Warsaw, I had knocked on the door of Rabbi Dov Pertzowicz who resided in the community building. Fearful and suspicious, he at first refused to let me in, until I somehow managed to assure him that I had no intention of harming him. I told him that I was an American rabbi who had come in search of his fellow Jews. *"Was zucht ir?"* he asked me. *"Ir vet gornicht gefinen."* "What are you looking for? You won't find anything."

Now, thirty years later, as I entered the unprepossessing building on Ulica Twarda 6, where the sole Jewish congregation of Warsaw is housed, I thought of Rabbi Pertzowicz--of the way his face had lit up with simple gratitude for being remembered when I had handed him a package of bandages from my friend, Rabbi Bronstein, who had instructed the new Warsaw *mohel* in the art of circumcision. Rabbi Pertzowicz is long gone, and this time, in May, 1990, as I came into the building, I was welcomed by Moses Finkelstein, the president of the Polish Jewish community. Mr. Finkelstein, a polite and engaging man, greeted me hospitably, pausing in his preparations for the imminent arrival from Israel of Rabbi Pinchas Menachem Joskowicz, who would serve as chief rabbi of Poland.

In addition to Moses Finkelstein, the Warsaw Jewish community is led by Dr. Pavel Wildstein and a secretary. (Until recently, this position was held by the late Michal Bjalkowicz.) These three dedicated souls, with the invaluable help of funding from the Joint Distribution

Committee, struggle to keep the community alive. Daily dinners are served in the community dining room to over one hundred Jews. The men wear yarmulkes as they eat. Kosher meat is provided by a *shochet* who arrives once a month from Budapest and spends two days slaughtering meat in Warsaw, Lodz, and Krakow; customers may purchase up to five pounds to last the month. This pattern of a small dedicated leadership, support from the Joint Distribution Committee, and a drastically limited availability of religious goods and services is repeated in several major cities in Poland, including Krakow, Lodz, Katowice, and others.

But apart from these organized efforts, there are pitifully few signs of Jewish life in Warsaw, whose 360,000 Jews had constituted, before the war, nearly a third of the city's population. It is sorrowful, indeed, to walk along the once Jewish streets of Warsaw--Nalewky, Gesia, Novolipky, and others--searching in vain for signs of Jewish life, for the great institutions of learnings, for the scholars and rabbis and merchants and students, for the men and women and children, who had once flourished there. Once a bustling, throbbing city, without its Jews Warsaw today seems gray and lifeless. Streams of people walk along the avenues, in and out of shops, under the watchful, slightly ominous eye of the city's tallest building, the Cultural Center erected as a gift from the Soviet Union to the Polish people. But where are the Jews? Even the few who remain cannot be distinguished from the general populace, so desperately do they strive to avoid appearing different and attracting attention to themselves.

One family I became acquainted with during this visit consisted of a Jewish mother, a Polish Catholic father, and four sons. None of the sons had been circumcised. The woman explained that her husband regarded circumcision as a violation of his Christian faith, and, for her part, the mother preferred that her sons remain uncircumcised to avoid detection as Jews. "What happened once can happen again," she said to me. "I want my sons to survive."

Indeed, intermarriage is widespread in Poland, and of the several hundred Jews remaining there, only a handful are married to fellow Jews. In general, the reasons given for this are the scarcity of Jews, a lifetime spent in a Christian society among Polish friends, and even, occasionally, a marriage to a Christian in gratitude for a life saved.

A highlight of Jewish community life in Warsaw is the monthly recorded cantorial concert at the city's only synagogue. These concerts are extremely popular with Jews and non-Jews alike, and tickets must be purchased well in advance. As I stood in the Warsaw synagogue, deeply moved by the powerful music and basking in the good-will the concert was fostering between Jews and their Polish neighbors, I remembered Cantor Sitkowsky, whom I had met on my first return visit to Poland. A middle-aged man, husky and out-going, Cantor Sitkowsky quickly began to show off his fine voice for my benefit. ''All I need is a chance,'' he said to me. ''You think Koussevitsky is great? Take me with you to America. I'll show you who's great!''

Chapter 3.
THE NEW RABBI

With the arrival from Israel of Rabbi Pinchas Menachem Joskowicz to serve as chief rabbi of Poland, a sense of renewal and hope surged through the Warsaw community. Originally from Zdunska Wola near Lodz, Rabbi Joskowicz had survived the war and several concentration camps. His mission to Poland marked his attempt to fulfill a vow he had taken long ago to exact revenge for what had been done to our people.

It had been a simple Jew called Rogozinsky who had charged Rabbi Joskowicz with the mission to exact revenge. During the Shavuot holiday of 1941 the Jews of Rabbi Joskowicz's town had been rounded up in the marketplace where gallows had been erected to hang a number of them chosen at random. Rogozinsky had been one of those selected. As he was led to the gallows, Rogozinsky cried out, "*Yidden, nemt nekama far unzer blut*!!"--"Jews, avenge our blood!"

For years Rabbi Joskowicz had sought to find a way to carry out Rogozinsky's last request. It was to honor Rogozinsky's dying words that Rabbi Joskowicz, at the behest of Rabbi Yechezkel Besser, of the Lauder Foundation, left the comfort of his home and family in Jerusalem and came to Poland. The best revenge against the murderers, Rabbi Joskowicz told me, would be a revitalization of Jewish life in Poland.

Though intimately familiar with Polish life and a fluent speaker of the Polish language, Rabbi Joskowicz faces a formidable task. With the remnants of Polish Jewry scattered throughout the country, it will be extremely difficult to provide the necessary services. But Rabbi Joskowicz is full of hope and optimism. As a soldier in the Israeli army, he told me, he learned that if there's a will, there's a way. He recalled how, as a young religious soldier, he had asked permission of his commanding officer to return home for a Shabbat on which no particular activity had been planned. A soldier must banish thoughts of home, the commanding officer had admonished the young Rabbi Joskowicz. Here in Poland, Rabbi Joskowicz assured me, his total attention would be focused on the task before him; all other thoughts would be banished. With the cooperation of Jewish groups and the Polish government, and with God's help, he would succeed.

Of course, Rabbi Joskowicz does not aspire to make Jewish Poland what it once was; nor does he seek to encourage Jews to return to Poland. In our conversations, Rabbi Joskowicz and I outlined a series of modest goals that required immediate attention:

- **The establishment of a daily morning and evening *minyan*:** If necessary, this could be carried out by offering a small monthly payment to ten or eleven men. However it is accomplished, a daily *minyan* adds essential purpose and dignity to a synagogue. The *minyan* would be available to Jewish guests from abroad who would no doubt contribute financially to its maintenance.
- **The hiring of a full-time *shochet*:** To insure the availability of kosher meat and poultry to all Jews who desire it, a ritual slaughterer must either be trained from among Poland's Jews or brought in from another country.
- **The organization of a *chevra kadisha* to provide Jewish burials for men and women:** Moreover, provision needed to be made to prevent the burial of Jews in non-Jewish cemeteries and vice versa. Indeed, during my visit to Poland, the administrators of the Jewish Gesia cemetery had approved the burial on its grounds of the gentile wife of a Jew. Since their approval could not be rescinded, I suggested that she be buried in a separate section where there were no graves and that in the future this area be fenced off from the rest of the cemetery and designated for such burials.
- **The opening of a strictly kosher restaurant:** Such a restaurant could serve either meat or dairy food, and would be heavily patronized by the many Jews who visit Poland.
- **The establishment of a *talmud torah*:** A place where men and women, young and old, could be taught the basics of Judaism, starting with the *alef-bet*, was sorely needed.

During the *kiddush* on Rabbi Joskowicz's first Shabbat in Warsaw I urged the members of his community to give him their full support and cooperation. The task before him is monumental. We must all pray that he will succeed.

Chapter 4.
THE RONALD S. LAUDER FOUNDATION

Much of the credit for engaging the services of Rabbi Joskowicz and for supporting and encouraging his activities belongs to the Lauder Foundation, established in 1987 by the philanthropist, Ronald S. Lauder. According to Mr. Lauder, the Foundation is "rooted in tradition and is respectful of our common heritage. It is my belief that through education--education of our holy landmarks--and the creation of worldwide linkages, we can eradicate the bigotry and hate which mar the past and cast shadows on the future. This is the challenge. This is the promise. And this will be the source of our success."

With the help of the Lauder Foundation, Rabbi Joskowicz has succeeded in organizing a daily *minyan* in addition to the existing Sabbath service. The Foundation has also been involved in establishing a kosher restaurant near the Warsaw synagogue, and a *mikvah* is now being completed in the synagogue's basement on Ulica Twarda 6. The refurbishing of the synagogue, and the revitalization of religious institutions for the first time in thirty years represent a major achievement of the Lauder Foundation, working closely with the Joint Distribution Committee.

In addition to these projects, the Lauder Foundation has also been involved in organizing kindergartens, operating summer camps, rebuilding Jewish cemeteries, preserving sacred remains, and restoring synagogues. But its paramount mission, as Mr. Lauder explains it, is education: "We are a link in a chain of education which reaches far into our history, and which must extend far into our future. After decades of repression, our work is now beginning.'' The Lauder kindergarten in Warsaw, in which I viewed about twenty children playing with the most up-to-date equipment in an atmosphere suffused with a love of Jewish learning, is one testament to the dedication to that mission. Another project now underway under the auspices of the Lauder Foundation is the construction of a youth center in the building of the Warsaw synagogue, which was shown to me with great pride by Petrick Tajdelczyk, and which will eventually attract young people who have never before identified with their Jewish background.

According to Rabbi Chaskel Besser, who, along with his younger colleague, Rabbi Michael Shudrich, serve as Lauder's special representatives to Polish Jewry, ''It is felt that across the former Iron Curtain countries there is a new generation just learning what it is to be free in thought, action, and faith. That kind of simple freedom had not been possible until now.'' Toward the goal of reaching these emerging Jews, the Lauder Foundation sponsors summer and winter retreats in Poland for Eastern European families, where instructors from the United States and Israel teach the fundamental aspects of Judaism, including Hebrew language, Jewish history, and kosher cooking. At these retreats, traditional Sabbath meals are served, enabling Polish Jews to experience the fulness and richness of their heritage.

Mrs. Grazyna Pawlak, supported by the Lauder Foundation, is generally credited with organizing these summer and winter retreats for children and adults. An ebullient and enthusiastic woman who claims descent from Chassidic grandparents, she is now the director of the Historical Institute of the Jewish People in Warsaw, and the leader and organizer of the Maccabee Club, which, she feels, will ''uncover'' Jews who have been ''hidden'' until now. Mrs. Pawlak asserts that there are now 500 registered Jews in Warsaw, but it is her belief that there are many others who refuse to identify as Jews. The Maccabee Club, sponsored by the Lauder Foundation, offers youth and sports centers, kindergartens, lectures, and others activities designed to reach out to alienated Jews.

According to Mrs. Pawlak, the first Lauder camp opened with only seven children. The following year, the camp was operated in Komarow near Warsaw, with fifty youngsters. Kosher meals were served, and, in addition to the regular camp activities, religious services were conducted. The Lauder camps quickly became extremely popular, and two more camps were soon opened with hundreds of children attending. Several of these young people returned home after the summer inspired by a new Jewish consciousness.

One of the stirring successes of the Lauder program is Basha Jakubowska, who attended a camp for twenty adults sponsored by the Foundation. Basha's father was Christian; she had been baptized as a child, attended church every Sunday, and enjoyed her annual Christmas tree. Her mother, however, refused to talk about her background, and Basha, for her part, always felt herself to be Jewish. Following her experiences at the Lauder Jewish camp, Basha was brought to the United States by Rabbi Besser with the help of the Foundation. In New York, she practiced Jewish law and ritual, and prepared for her conversion at the Drisha Institute. The day of her orthodox conversion to Judaism was the happiest in her life, Basha recalls. The Lauder Foundation then assisted Basha in finding work as a teacher with the goal of eventually returning to Poland to find other lost Jewish children and restoring them to Jewish life and tradition.

The Krakow representative of the Lauder Foundation, a tall, bearded, intelligent man who spoke English quite well and even some Hebrew, also expressed himself with great pride on the subject of his organization's accomplishments. The Foundation, he told me, is cooperating with experts from the United States and Poland to make certain that the remaining evidence of former concentration camp sites not be obliterated by time or by human interference. Together, we traveled to Auschwitz to visit the new structure now completed and designed to house the nuns about 700 meters from the contested Carmelite convent.

The new, so-called "Educational Center," is directed by a priest, Father Marek Glownia, who gave us a grand tour of the establishment, which will consist of four parts: a meeting hall, a pilgrims' hostel, the administration and service building, and the convent. He also handed us a brochure, which describes the mandate of the center in this way: "The center organizes meetings, courses, seminars, and congresses, creating opportunities for dialogue between people of different nationalities, religions, and convictions. It seeks to foster better mutual enrichment, especially among the young people of Europe. It seeks, in particular, to facilitate the study of the culture and the fates of the Jewish people who made up about 90 percent of the victims of the Auschwitz death factory."

In the shadow of this new center, Auschwitz stands, silent and unforgiving. The signs of the destruction wrought there and in other such places are still starkly evident throughout Europe. The pitiful remains of the Jewish community in Poland is one of the most terrible legacies, and it is for the sake of this remnant that the Lauder Foundation has so generously and effectively organized its energies and resources.

Chapter 5.
ZIGMUNT NISSENBAUM

Among the worshippers welcoming Rabbi Joskowicz on his first Sabbath in Warsaw was Zigmunt Nissenbaum. His story, which he related to me during a three-hour conversation that evening at the Victoria Intercontinental Hotel, closely parallels, in many of its horrifying details, the story of Warsaw Jewry.

Zigmunt Nissenbaum was only twelve years old when the war broke out. He lived with his family on Grzybowska Street. As a young boy he witnessed what no child--indeed, no human being--should ever have had to see: families freezing to death in wintertime; people dropping from starvation on the pavement, in yards, on staircases; human being reduced to the lowest level, robbed of all dignity and hope. While the Jews of Warsaw and the surrounding areas were squeezed into the ghetto, Nissenbaum and a group of friends hid out in the Brodno Cemetery. And though the Nazis patrolled there, he and his companions found solace among the family tombstones. During the first month of using this hideout, Nissenbaum watched in terror as a rabbi carrying a Torah scroll was executed. The sight etched itself into his memory. He would never forget it.

Nissenbaum was taken to the *Umschlagplatz* three times. The Nazis called this short, cobbled road with the railway platform at its end the *Himmelfahrstrasse*, the Street to Heaven. For the 500,000 Jews driven there and prodded with rifle butts into the chloride-soaked cattle wagons for the trip to Treblinka, it was the final street, the last road.

...lagplatz for the first time in ...ghetto without an arm band. ...ight outside without his arm ...As the freight cars were being ...some sort. The Nazi guards ...m managed to escape. ...the *Umschlagplatz*.. He had ...d explosives in a prearranged ...ing. This time he was closely ...ar the door. The S.S. ordered ...en searched them at random, ...ods were found. Dead bodies ...car. Nissenbaum hid under ...them by cart to the cemetery. ...overed with the blood of the ...a pit, filling it only halfway ...aum rose from the grave and

...arsaw Ghetto, Nissenbaum ...st time. The Nazis had set the ...ws inside were forced to flee ...hem from below. The smoke ...senbaum wet a handkerchief ...o his mother. On one of the rooftops they found a girl who had been shot in the legs while fighting on Mila Street. They dragged her by the hands and descended the stairs of one of the buildings. As they attempted to cross over into an adjacent building they were caught by the Nazis. Nissenbaum's brother leaped into a burning house as the soldiers shot at him. Later he was taken to Majdanek where he perished.

At the *Umschlagplatz* they were stripped of their valuables and the shooting was renewed. Nissenbaum's mother urged him to flee. The wounded girl from Mila Street collapsed. An SS man put a gun to her head and shot. The bullet left a hole in the ground, but the girl, moaning and moving her hands, was still alive. A second SS man came up and shot her dead. The cold-blooded murder of this girl was a sight that Nissenbaum would never forget.

They were sealed inside the freight cars, children crammed in over their heads, standing eighteen hours before the train even began to move. Three days later they arrived at Treblinka. By that time, half the passengers were already dead.

At Treblinka, Nissenbaum's father and eighty others were detached from the transport to be used as slave laborers. Nissenbaum, along with the remaining men, women, children, and the elderly, were pushed toward the gas chambers. At the last moment, Nissenbaum spotted a wheelbarrow loaded with eyeglasses and other small objects. He grabbed the wheelbarrow and pushed it toward his father's group. Nobody noticed, and Nissenbaum's life was saved.

From Treblinka, Nissenbaum was shipped to the Majdanek labor camp in Lublin, then to the salt mines in Wieliczka, then to Auschwitz, a POW camp in Budzyn, back again to Majdanek, a penal camp in Flossenberg inside Germany, forced labor in Herzberg, again to Flossenberg, later Offenberg near the French border, and finally escaping from Offenberg and joining French forces preparing an offensive against the Germans.

After the war, Nissenbaum settled in Constance, West Germany, near the Swiss border. There he prospered. He bought a shipyard and helped found a community consisting of Polish Jews. He built a private synagogue, which he dedicated to his parents. For nearly forty years he could not bear to return to Poland. Then, six years ago, he went back and visited the family graves in the Brodno Cemetery, which he found desecrated beyond imagination.

Nissenbaum's three trips to the *Umschlagplatz* would never be forgotten. The *Umschlagplatz* Memorial commemorates the martyrdom of the 300,000 Jews who were collected at that spot and transported from there to the Treblinka death camp where they were annihilated. This memorial is a project of the Nissenbaum Foundation.

As more and more Jews visit Poland in search of their lost childhoods, their families and their origins, the cemeteries constitute a vital link to their past. Some years ago, hundreds of tombstones that had been removed by the Nazis from the Warsaw Jewish cemetery and used to pave roads and sidewalks were found in a building at Ulica Dworkowa 7. Many of these stones were returned to the cemetery and an appropriate service was conducted.

Nissenbaum recounted an astonishing event that occurred recently. Not long ago, a construction company bought a parcel of land that had, in 1942, been the site upon which ten thousand Jews were made to dig ditches and then were shot by the Nazis. Subsequently, this site had been used as a soccer stadium. When the construction company began digging the foundation of the building it struck human remains: skulls, skeletons, and limbs. Nevertheless, the company refused to curtail its work until Polish neighbors protested. When Nissenbaum was informed of this matter he went directly to Polish authorities who issued a restraining order against the company.

Then Nissenbaum brought in rabbis from the United States, Great Britain, and Israel to determine what to do with the remains. He showed me photographs of rabbis collecting bones and holding in their hands human skulls. He was determined to accord burial to each skull as if it were a complete person. Approximately five hundred coffins were brought in and a skull was placed in each; separate coffins were used for the limbs. All of these remains were interred with full religious honors. The entire field was declared a *makom kadosh*, a holy place, and a large monument is now being erected in memory of these martyrs. Priests and bishops attended the burial ceremony in full dress, displaying crosses on their chests. When Nissenbaum explained to these Christian clergymen the rabbis' objection to this display, the priests and bishops covered their crosses with their coats, donned skull caps, and respectfully stood and witnessed the entire ceremony.

Chapter 6.
LUBLIN

Nachum Ziviak, a seventy-two year old resident of Twarda 6 in Warsaw with a long-lost brother in New York, was delighted when I offered him a ride to Lublin. He hadn't been there for a long time and it was indeed a privilege to once again have the opportunity to visit the grave of the Chozeh of Lublin, as well as the building where Rabbi Meyer Shapiro had headed the Yeshiva Chachmei Lublin.

Our driver was familiar with all the communities in the area. When I asked him to stop at some of the many towns and villages we were passing along the way, he informed us that that there were no longer any Jews there, nor were there synagogues. The cemeteries, too, had all been demolished, and monuments and tombstones had been removed from the graveyards to be used to pave roads. There were no Jews in Pilawa, Otwock, Garwolin, Zelechow, or Ryki. Nor where there Jews in Kock or Radzyn. The sorrowful litany went on. The driver took us directly to Lublin.

Nachum Ziviak knew of one person in Lublin who still retained some interest in his Jewish heritage. When we reached Lublin, Ziviak knew exactly where to locate this *parasolnik*, this umbrella maker--a first floor apartment on Ulica Slavinskiego 3. The *parasolnik*, Nachum Schicz, was married to a Russian woman whom he swore was Jewish. "I'm not like the others," he declared. "I went to a rabbi and got married. I can even show you my marriage certificate." Schicz is a man with a long beard who says that he owns a *tallit* and *tefilin* and that he prays daily. He and his wife both speak fluent Yiddish.

It took a while for Schicz's natural distrust of strangers to ease. "Walls have ears," he asserted. But in time he began to open up to me. He claimed to be a poet and writer, and even showed me some of his work in Polish. Eventually he agreed to guide us through what remains of Jewish Lublin.

At Lubartowska 10 a former house of worship had been converted into a museum. The door was open when we arrived, and six people were having a meeting, discussing museum business. A younger member of the group explained to us that when there were no longer enough people to conduct religious services, a decision had been made to turn the building into a museum. There was an ark and a table in the center of the room, and some bookcases containing old, torn Hebrew volumes. A photograph of Rabbi Meyer Shapiro hung on one wall, as well as depictions of Jewish life in Lublin before and during the war. There was no Torah, and very few prayer books or *chumashim*.. Schicz told me that he went to Warsaw to pray on the High Holidays.

On our way out of the museum we met a Pole who was trying to sell some badly torn Hebrew books for 10,000 zlotys. Schicz offered him 200, but the offer was refused. There was no deal. The Poles think these *shaymes* are treasures and periodically try to sell them to the only Jew in town.

We then made our way to the site of Rabbi Meyer Shapiro's *Yeshiva Chachmei Lublin*, which is now a Polish university that appears to be neglected both inside and out. The only sign that this building once housed a yeshiva are some architectural details on the facade. The director of the university was cordial and polite, and escorted us through the building to view the classrooms and study halls. Only one *mezuzah* indentation on an interior doorpost indicated the former presence of a yeshiva. The director explained that the entire structure is being remodeled and refurbished.

Schicz led us to a monument (*pomnik*) on the site where the Lublin Ghetto once stood. He insisted that I hear the Lublin story from him. In 1939, there were 38,000 Jews in Lublin. The Yeshiva Chachmei Lublin had been opened in 1923 with Rabbi Shapiro serving at its head until 1933. After that there was no chief rabbi in Lublin, only a *bet din* consisting of three rabbis who officiated over all religious functions. On September 18, 1939, the Nazis captured Lublin and began to deport its Jews to forced labor camps. By the end of March, 1941, 34,000 Jews were packed inside the Lublin Ghetto. Beginning March 16, 1942, 1,500 Jews were evacuated from the ghetto daily. Thirty thousand

Lublin Jews were murdered in Belzec and 4,000 in Mido Tatarsky. On September 2, 1942, 2,000 Lublin Jews were murdered; at the end of October another 1,800 were wiped out, and 200 were sent to Maidanek. In May, 1943, all the remaining Jews of Lublin were deported to Maidanek.

During the war, Schicz told me, there was an underground unit operating in the Lublin area led by Yechiel Greenspan. This group entered Lublin on July 24, 1944, after the Russian army liberated the city. Lublin became the temporary capital of Poland until January, 1945, when Warsaw was taken by the Russians. Thousands of repatriated Jews returned to Lublin, but most of these came from Russia. Anti-Semitism flared up again, and Jews left the city between 1946 and 1950. The final exodus of Jews from Lublin took place in 1968.

From the Lublin Ghetto Schicz led us to the old Jewish cemetery. The grave of the Chozeh of Lublin, he told us, is visited by thousands of Jews from around the world. The Jewish leadership of Warsaw, Schicz informed us, had recently signed over the new Lublin cemetery to the Polish government for conversion into a park.

A new structure was rising in front of the cemetery. This was the work of Belgian Jews, Schicz said; the building was intended for use as a synagogue and a museum. Assuring me once again that his wife is Jewish, that he puts on *tefilin* daily and that he goes along with other Jews to Warsaw for the High Holidays, Schicz took his leave and we departed from the city of Lublin, once a hub of Jewish activity and now bereft.

Below: Chief Rabbi
of Poland
Pinchas Menachem Joskowitz
with author

Above: Vishnitzer Chasidim
visiting Auschwitz Camp

Below: Chief Rabbi Joskowitz

Right: Ovens in Majdanek

1930   1990

Above: Budynek b. "JESZIWAS CHACHMEJ LUBLIN" (WYZSZA UCZELNIA RABINACKA) Building of the former YESHIVA CHACHMEJ LUBLIN (Rabbinical Academy). Today Polish Medical School

Left: "Never Again" Monument at Treblinka

Above: Chief Rabbi Israel Low of Israel speaks to visitors at Treblinka

R. Moses Isserles
c.1520-1572

Left: The REMA

Chapter 7.
MAJDANEK

At noon we arrived at Majdanek, six miles from the center of Lublin. The camp is now a well-kept museum to which hundreds of visitors come daily. On display are huge showcases filled with mountains of shoes, clothing, valises, women's hair. A round, umbrella-shaped roof has recently been installed over a large area piled with human ashes. An attached sign tells the story: "Here the ashes of the victims of the camp are deposited." The gas chambers in which thousands of people were asphyxiated are also on view. The sign says: "Twenty-five nations were victims here, among them Russians and Jews." Another sign inside the camp gives this information: "On the third of November 1943, 18,400 Jews were shot in this place." How could a single visitor take all of this in? I recited a chapter of *Tehilim* and a *Molei* in memory of the dead.

Majdanek was set up by the Germans in 1941 to serve as a camp for the internment of prisoners of war. Soon after, Jews were transported there from Czechoslovakia, France, and Greece. In the spring of 1942 gas chambers and crematoria were built and Jews from Poland were brought to Majdanek, particularly from the areas of Warsaw and Bialystok.

According to the museum guide at Majdanek, the transports of Polish Jews who were brought to the camp in early 1942 were part of what was called "Action Reinhard." Three thousand Lublin Jews were selected for immediate execution. On April 20, 1942, they were forced to march to Majdanek from the nearby ghetto in Majdan Tatarsky. The entire group spent the first night in three or four stables. The SS selected between two and three hundred men they deemed fit for work and moved them to the camp. The rest--women, children, the aged and the infirm--were taken in trucks to a forest about twelve kilometers from Majdanek, in the direction of Lvov. There they were stripped of their clothing and possessions and shot to death.

Two weeks later camp leaders selected 2,500 people sick with typhus and marched them to Compound Three. That night, they were transported to Krepiecki Forest and shot. This was how the Nazis cured typhus at Majdanek.

I asked the guide for details about the sign I had noticed: the shooting of the 18,400 Jews on November 3, 1943. This particular operation was known as *"Erntefest,"* he told us, "Harvest Festival." In the autumn of 1943, the Nazis were greatly concerned about the uprisings in the Warsaw and Bialystok ghettos, as well as about the rebellions in the death camps of Sobibor and Treblinka. Himmler ordered the liquidation of all the Jews in the Lublin area.

In October, 1943, three hundred Jews were divided into two groups and set to work in twelve-hour shifts digging ditches. SS men began to arrive from Auschwitz, Krakow, Warsaw, Radom, Lvov, and Lublin-- a total of about one hundred officers known as *Sonderkommandos*. On the night of November 2, two trucks equipped with loudspeakers were brought into the camp; one was placed at the entrance and the other alongside the ditches.

That night thousands of Jews were forced out of the barracks. Police dogs sniffed out those who attempted to flee or to hide. Men and women were stripped naked and taken in separate groups of one hundred to the ditches. Music blasted from the trucks' loudspeakers. The condemned passed between the rows of SS men who shoved them into the ditches in groups of ten. They were forced to lie down as the *Sonderkommandos* shot them. Then the next groups of ten was forced to lie on top of the corpses, and they, too, were shot. This action continued from seven in the morning, barely interrupted at five in the afternoon when the exhausted first shift of Nazis went off to dinner and was replaced by fresh murderers. The action was carried out to the accompaniment of the trucks' music until the ditches were filled and over 18,000 Jews were dead, men and women in separate ditches.

That day--November 3, 1943--became known as "Bloody Wednesday." In addition to the 18,400 killed at Majdanek, another 18,000 were murdered at Poniatowa, and 10,000 at Trawniki. November

3, 1943 was also a black day for the Jews at Majdanek who survived the massacre, many of whom became depressed and apathetic as a similar fate seemed to loom over them.

The number of human beings processed by the Nazi killing machine in a single day was simply staggering. During the war, over a quarter of a million Jews perished in Majdanek, the guide said.

Chapter 8.
ON THE ROAD TO TREBLINKA

My companion during the journey to Treblinka was a Warsaw Jew who was born during the war and spent his earliest years in a Christian home. His father was killed in the Warsaw Ghetto uprising. His mother survived the war and was remarried afterward to a devout Catholic. Though my companion was reared in this Catholic environment, he was still subjected to racial insults from Polish children at school and he was also spurned by the handful of Jewish children who had remained in Poland and who treated him contemptuously because he appeared to have abandoned his faith. No longer able to tolerate this atmosphere, he ran away as a teenager. His interest in Judaism grew as he read and studied, and he even occasionally visited a synagogue. However, he married a Polish woman and they agreed not to impose any religion on their three children. He now makes his living as a guide primarily to Jewish visitors to Poland.

Some years ago, he had served as a guide to an American couple who had lost a father, mother, and three children in the Holocaust. A surviving child had been placed in a Catholic institution for disturbed children. This child had been diagnosed as traumatized as a result of his circumcision, and the nuns never let him out of their sight. After considerable investigation, the American couple was finally able to locate the whereabouts of the missing child, who had now become the beneficiary of an estate worth over $100,000. However, the boy was declared incompetent, incapable of handling the money, and it was turned over to the church. The American couple was never able to retrieve the boy from his Christian "protectors."

My guide told me that more than a decade after the war, there were still about 2,000 Jewish children living in gentile homes, monasteries, or churches in the Warsaw area. Over half of these were lost to the Jewish people either because Jewish relatives refused to take them in, or the children themselves refused to leave the only home they remembered, or the gentiles would not give them up, or the church would not allow anyone near them or would claim that the parents of the children had forsaken them and did not care about them anyway. When questioned on this matter, however, the Jewish leadership in Poland asserts that everything that could have been done to resolve this problem, was done.

Not that long ago, there was a successful case brought by a Jewish boy against his adoptive Polish parents who sought to prevent him from returning to his roots. With the help of Jewish groups, the boy took his "parents" to court and won three times as his parents appealed all the way up to the highest tribunal. The boy left Poland and went to study in England, where he became extremely pious and an outstanding student. Of course, the necessary ingredient in this case was that the boy himself was deeply committed to returning to his faith.

We continued to discuss these and similar topics until we reached Treblinka, 65 miles from Warsaw. The death camp known as Treblinka was in operation less than eighteen months, from July 1942 to November 1943, yet during that brief period 800,000 people were murdered there, mostly Jews from Warsaw, Germany, Bulgaria, and Greece. Every effort was made by the Nazis to camouflage the nefarious purpose of the camp. Deep in a forest, Treblinka was equipped with a picturesque train platform, complete with restaurant and waiting room. When their evil work was done, the Nazis destroyed the camp, but for many years articles of clothing, valises, and even human limbs and ashes could be found strewn about the area.

From the picturesque station, groups of twenty cars loaded with Jews would be brought to a side track. As they were rushed out of the cars, the prisoners were beaten by German and Ukrainian guards; those who lingered were shot on the spot. Yet inside the camp, things appeared quite ordinary: a Red Cross flag was displayed to indicate the location of the hospital; there were waiting rooms with sofas and chairs. All of this was designed to distract and calm the children, the invalids and the elderly, who were led through a door to the edge of a pit, and shot in the back of the head. The pit that received these victims was also the final resting place of those who had died on the trip or at the station.

In the station, Jews were ordered to surrender their valuables, such as gold and silver, which were immediately sent to Germany. According to recorded information, 203 wagonloads of clothing alone reached Germany from Treblinka. Then the victims were ordered to undress. They were chased naked with whips and guns to the gas chambers, their hands raised to make more room for others. The doors were sealed and exhaust pipes from captured Soviet tanks released carbon monoxide into the chambers until everyone inside was dead. When the doors were opened and the poison gas subsided, a special crew, known as the ''dentists,'' entered to extract the gold teeth from the mouths of the dead. The bodies were then thrown into the pit for burning.

Ivan the Terrible was said to have stood at the entrance to the gas chamber at Treblinka and to have viciously pushed the inmates inside. Yaakov Viernuk, a survivor of Treblinka who testified at the trial of John Demjanjuk in Jerusalem, described the Ukrainian officer in this way: ''Ivan had pleasant but sadistic eyes. The pain and suffering of the inmates seemed to give him special pleasure. At times he attacked us and would use nails to nail our ears to the wall.''

On August 2, 1943, the inmates of Treblinka, after weeks of preparation, rose in rebellion against their persecutors. When it became clear that all was lost, their leader, Dr. Chozorowsky, swallowed poison, but a particularly sadistic guard known as Franz sought to revive him by prying his mouth open with a knife and pouring water down his throat. All this was done in order to inflict an even crueller death on the rebellion leader, but fortunately, the doctor was already dead. A number of SS officers and many Ukrainian guards were killed during the revolt, and 300 prisoners escaped. The barracks were set on fire. Most of those who had managed to escaped were betrayed by local peasants, but some were given refuge and hidden.

As a result of this rebellion, the Nazis determined to shut down the camp. Beginning on the day of the revolt, the Nazis burned all the corpses. In October 1943, all the buildings at Treblinka were blown up by the Nazis and the camp was ploughed under to hide every trace of its existence. By November, the extermination camp with its two gas chambers was demolished. The penal labor camp, however, known as Treblinka I, which had been in operation since 1941, continued until July 1944. The last recorded murders took place there on July 24, 1944, just before the arrival of the Russians.

Nothing remains of Treblinka where nearly one million souls perished. To memorialize this terrible place, the Polish government erected a granite monument resembling a tombstone surrounded by 17,000 jagged rocks to symbolize the men and women who had been killed by the Nazis at Treblinka.

Chapter 9.
LODZ

Michael Nadel, an attorney who practices law in Lodz, serves as the representative of the Jewish community. An elegant gentleman, Nadel informed me that there are now almost 600 Jews in Lodz, of whom 115 identify with the community. The rest are either assimilated or too frightened to identify strongly as Jews. The intermarriage rate is nearly 100 percent; the number of Jewish couples can almost be counted on the fingers of one hand. There are very few young Jews in Lodz and no bar-mitzvahs or weddings are celebrated there. The *shochet* arrives from Budapest once a month to slaughter some chickens and cows. Since there is no *mohel* at all in Poland, many of the boys are circumcised at birth by a doctor. There were two synagogues in Lodz but one burned down recently. Religious services are now held at Ulica Zachodnia 78, only on Saturday and holiday mornings, with a *minyan* that consists of between ten and fifteen men. The cemetery is kept in good order.

Nadel has a yeshiva background. He urged me to send his good wishes to the Mossad Ha'Rav Kook in Jerusalem and to remind Dr. Yitzchak Rafael that he had sat beside him in *cheder* in Lemberg and that both of them had been part of the Bnei Akiva movement in Lvov. A pleasant man, Nadel nevertheless has some disturbing religious views. He strongly disagreed with me when I informed him that the children of a non-Jewish wife are not *halachically* regarded as Jewish. ''By you in America and in Israel that's true,'' he told me. ''But here in Poland a non-Jewish woman who goes to *shul* and lights candles on

Friday night is considered a Jewess and she is entitled to be buried next to her husband in a Jewish cemetery. If this couple has children who are raised as Jews, they are automatically Jewish.'' I tried in vain to persuade him otherwise. At this point I did not dare ask if his wife is Jewish.

At the outbreak of the war, there were approximately a quarter of a million Jews in Lodz. This was where the great *Gaon*, Rabbi Eliyahu Chaim Meisels, lived. The city was a center of Jewish activity, scholarship, and institutions of learnings. After the Germans entered Lodz on September 8, 1939, about one-third of its Jewish population fled to Warsaw or followed the Russian army. The Nazis burned down the city's largest synagogue and publicly hanged several of its Jewish leaders. In December 1939, Jews were evicted from their homes, which were occupied by Germans. On February 8, 1941, the Lodz Ghetto was officially opened by the Nazis and 164,000 Jews were incarcerated inside.

The leader of the ghetto, Mordechai Chaim Rumkowski, known as the ''Elder of the Jews,'' was a remarkably "competent" administrator. As late as August 1942, there were 91 factories operating inside the ghetto, employing 78,000 workers. There were seven hospitals, five pharmacies, and several infirmaries. There was an educational board that oversaw 45 religious and non-religious schools. There were two high schools and one trade school, two old-age homes, orphanages, homes for the chronically ill, and children's camps. There were courts and a prison system. There was also a committee in charge of directing the agricultural activities of the ghetto, primarily vegetable gardens.

Invaluable insight into the activities of the Lodz Ghetto can be obtained from the recorded diaries, which were meticulously maintained on a daily basis:
1.   On February 23, 1941, the remains of a child in total decay were uncovered in the building at 42 Francziskanska, covered with rags. The doctor who was summoned to the scene could not give the precise date of death but estimated it at two weeks previous to the visit. The child's father, Hersh Aragur, a *badchan* [wedding entertainer], did not initially wish to disclose his reason for not burying his only son, seven years old, but later confessed that he had done so in order to use his bread and food coupons. The father was arrested.

2. Tzvaiga Blum, a forty-one year old resident of 21 Limanowski
    Street, was shot to death near the barbed wire of the ghetto at the end
    of Brzezinska Street. The victim was suffering from mental illness
    and had just been released from the mental institution on Wesola
    Street. According to witnesses, the unfortunate woman had walked
    up to the barbed wire several times to request that the sentries shoot
    her. She had been denied her request several times, but on that
    fateful day the sentry had ordered her to dance in front of the barbed
    wire. As a payment for her entertainment, he shot her dead at point
    blank range.

3. A pail of soup was carried up two flights to the Loan Fund Office
    at 17 Zgierska Street. The woman carrying it was jostled and some
    of the soup with diced potatoes spilled on the steps. Behind her was
    a man dragging himself up the steps to request a loan and he was
    tired and could hardly get from one step to the other. When he spied
    the spilled soup his eyes filled with tears: ''Soup on the stairs.'' He
    didn't pause to think. Instead, he pulled out the spoon which every
    ghetto dweller always carried. He sat down on the step and spooned
    the soup from the filthy step, forgetting completely why he was
    there--to obtain a loan. There was no fear that the steps were filthy
    and he may become ill; he already knows he is immune to typhoid.
    The few drops of soup cannot satisfy him, but he can't help it. He
    is hungry.

4. The only two happy days in the ghetto occurred first on Yom
    Kippur, which was a day marked by dignity and solemnity. People
    walked silently through the street in their ''best'' clothes, even the
    children. No *trepkis* [clogs] were seen. The boys wore ironed shirts;
    there were no bare feet. The girls wore ironed dresses and every one
    appeared well groomed. Once again families could get together as
    they had not been able to for a long time. Parents went strolling with
    the children hand-in-hand. On that day the workshops did not even
    keep husband and wife apart. Here and there one could see a Jew
    carrying a *sefer* Torah through the streets of the ghetto without
    hesitation. He was apparently going to some house which they had
    designated for services. In brief, Yom Kippur in Lodz in 1943
    turned the ghetto into a live ''*shtetl.* '' There was even a *yom-tov*
    dish on the table in the community kitchens where *cholent* was
    being dished out. In High German, they called it ''*Gedamfte
    Kartoflen.*''

The second happy day was Saturday, July 15, 1944, when the ghetto was overjoyed. On this day, the "Elder of the Ghetto" was instructed to halt the resettlement. Jews embraced in the street and kissed the workshops. "The resettlement is over." No one believed it would be a brief interruption or even a final halt to the transports. One thing is certain--no transport is being readied for Monday. The ghetto Jew had lost the ability to think more than a few hours ahead. At first some of the people refused to believe the news. After so much sorrow, one is reluctant to believe good tidings. Gradually, however, the Jews in the ghetto gained confidence and the feeling of happiness and relief ·vas shared by all.

In April 1942, the Nazis forced 940 Jews from the Lodz Ghetto to the death camp Chelmno. The following month the Nazis deported another 11,000 Jews to Chelmno, not including children under the age of ten, elders over sixty, and the sick, for a total of 16,000 innocents sent to their deaths. By September 1942, only 90,000 Jews remained in the Lodz Ghetto. In August 1943, 90 percent of those left in the ghetto, including children as young as eight, were put to work in factories and on projects. In effect, the ghetto itself became a forced labor camp. The Lodz Ghetto was liquidated in August 1944, when the last 77,000 Jews were transferred to Auschwitz.

When the Soviet army entered Lodz in January 1945, they found only 800 Jews. After the war, Jews began returning to Lodz. By 1946, Lodz had the largest Jewish community in Poland, with a population of 50,000, mostly refugees from Russia. The Jewish community attempted to reorganize, forming institutions, opening theaters, bringing out publications, including newspapers in Polish, Yiddish, and Hebrew. There were also *hachsharot* programs for those preparing to go to Palestine. From 1946-1950, half the returning Jews left Lodz, and most of the remainder departed for Israel in 1965-1967 as a result of the difficult circumstances in Poland and the vigorous *aliyah* activities of the Israeli government. The few who remained sought to reorganize by forming schools and developing other activities, but with little success. Today, Lodz is a pale, lifeless shadow of the vibrant center of Jewish life that once was, that was savagely extinguished, that is no more.

Chapter 10.
PIOTRKOW

There are no Jews in Piotrkow. "*Niema Zhydy*," was the far from friendly reply of the Piotrkow chief of police when I inquired about the whereabouts of the city's Jews: No Jews.

I went to Piotrkow, a city of 600,000 inhabitants and not a single Jew, to honor my friend and colleague, Rabbi Israel Mayer Lau, chief rabbi of Israel. Piotrkow is Rabbi Lau's native city. This is where his learned father studied and taught, and it was from this city that Rabbi Lau's father went to his death in the Holocaust.

Some thirty miles from Lodz and about seventy miles from Warsaw along well-paved roads, Piotrkow in central Poland is considered part of the province of Lodz. It is an industrial city, with breweries, tanneries, flour mills, sawmills, and agricultural machinery parts. One of the oldest populated centers of Poland, it is the city in which, during the fifteenth and sixteenth centuries, the elections of the Polish kings were held. In the sixteenth century, anti-Jewish laws were passed in Piotrkow instigated by the Jesuits. In 1538, for example, a law was passed prohibiting Jews from engaging in agricultural work, and ordering them to wear distinctive garments to separate them from the Christians. Almost all of Piotrkow's Jewish families were slaughtered during the Cossack uprising of 1648, and no Jew was allowed to enter the city until 1679, when King John Sobiesky permitted them to return and build a synagogue.

In 1730, the Jews of Piotrkow, under the leadership of Rabbi Eliakim Getz, organized a *bikkur cholim* society to tend the sick and a *chevra kadisha* to bury the dead. With the installation of a new printing press, the *Talmud Yerushalmi* was published in Piotrkow and the city became an important center of Jewish scholarship. In 1918, when the independence of Poland was declared, the city of Piotrkow held elections for its municipal council; seven of the 33 members were Jewish. Until 1931, Rabbi Meir Shapiro served as spiritual leader of Piotrkow. He was followed in this position by the father of Rabbi Israel Lau, who served until the outbreak of the Second World War.

As soon as the war started, 2,000 young Jews fled Piotrkow for the Russian zone. On October 28, 1939, less than two months after the start of the war, Piotrkow became the first Polish city to establish a ghetto. By October 15, 1942, the population of the city had reached its peak of 25,000 Jews, about 50 percent of whom had come to Piotrkow from the surrounding towns and villages. One week later the Nazis deported 22,000 Piotrkow Jews to Treblinka where they were murdered. In May 1943, forty women and children were shot to death as a group of 500 Jews were being taken to the camps of Radom and Starachowice. A wall in present-day Piotrkow marks the place where the forty were killed. In November 1944, the final group of 1,000 Piotrkow Jews were deported to Buchenwald and Bergen-Belsen.

It was to Bucheuwald that my friend, Rabbi Herschel Schachter of the Bronx, came at the end of the war as part of the American forces liberating Europe. There he found two young Jewish boys among the very few who had survived the war. One of these boys was Naftali Lavie, now a distinguished officer in the Israeli government. The second child was Naftali's brother, Israel Mayer Lau, son of the Rabbi of Piotrkow and, today, chief rabbi of Israel.

Chapter 11.
THE MONUMENTS IN BYTOM

Few monuments or tombstones can be found in Poland to commemorate the life--the existence and passing--of individual Jews who were murdered there. There are no individual graves for the Jews exterminated in masses, and no single place on earth to which survivors can go to remember their loved ones. But in Bytom west of Krakow monuments were erected in the Jewish cemetery to mark the place where 38 Dutch Jews were laid to rest. Each monument records the name of the deceased, his date of birth, and the date on which he was murdered.

Throughout the war until 1945, Bytom, a city that was once on the German-Polish border, was fully in German hands. The city's first Jewish cemetery was laid out in the 1730s; its first synagogue was erected in 1810, and another was built in 1870. There were only seven Jews in Bytom until 1784, but by 1935 there were 3,500, and the city boasted a religious school as well as a Jewish elementary school. As a result of Hitler's ascension to power in nearby Germany, about half of Bytom's Jews had already fled the city by the time the Nazis invaded Poland in September 1939. In 1942, 1,000 Jews, many of whom had arrived to Bytom from other places, were deported from that city to Auschwitz, where they perished.

In 1943, 38 Dutch Jews who had fled Holland and sought refuge in Bytom were murdered by the Nazis. Miraculously, they were laid to rest in graves clearly marked with their names, birth and death dates. Since this simple dignity was so rarely accorded to Jewish victims during the war years, it is fitting that we remember them:

Bornszstjn, Aaron (March 20, 1925 - February 28, 1943)
Cohen, Martinus (September 9, 1905 - March 7, 1943)
Davidson, Isaac (September 16, 1897 - September 30, 1943)
de Stolla, Louis (November 3, 1891 - April 9, 1943)
de Wilde, David (August 15, 1894 - March 14, 1943)
Gotlieb, Jacques Israel (May 1, 1897 - May 5, 1943)
Haas, Nathan Meir (July 31, 1897 - April 30, 1943)
Kleekoper, Nathan Levie (June 11, 1917 - March 31, 1943)
Kropveld, Jonas (November 29, 1919 - March 31, 1943)
Leverpoll, Simon (April 20, 1897 - July 31, 1943)
Lion, Silo Ernst (November 20, 1908 - May 13, 1943)
Lisser, Lion Hartog (February 2, 1925 - March 26, 1943)
Meinzer, Heinrich (January 10, 1908 - May 13, 1943)
Meuleman, Gerson (November 11, 1905 - March 7, 1943)
Meijer, Benno (August 16, 1899 - March 5, 1943)
Nof, Jacob (April 15, 1894 - October 31, 1943)
Nabarro, Hijman (May 20, 1896 - May 4, 1943)
Ossendriver (March 21, 1911 - March 12, 1943)
Phillips, Abrahaam (November 24, 1893 - April 12, 1943)
Prins, Simon Emanuel (September 19, 1893 - April 29, 1943)
Rintel, Emanuel Jacob (July 9, 1903 - May 4, 1943)
Rosenbaum, Walter (February 2, 1908 - March 20, 1943)
Rosendaal, Leonard (November 18, 1918 - March 16, 1918)
Schijveschuurder, Isaac (June 13, 1886 - April 15, 1943)
Sloog, Herman Louis (November 22, 1903 - November, 1943)
Sternfeld, Isaac (January 20, 1895 - April 20, 1943)
Theebom, Daniel (February 18, 1893 - March 24, 1943)
Trijtel, Joseph (November 7, 1897 - March 25, 1943)
van Dam, Aron (December 14, 1897 - April 30, 1943)
van Dam, Guilielmus (November 8, 1910 - March 19, 1943)
van Dam, Isak (Febraury 15, 1925 - January 4, 1943)
van Dantsich, Hartog (February 3, 1898 - April 6, 1943)
van Frank, Salomon (June 30, 1906 - October 2, 1943)
van Goor, Abraham Nathan (June 11, 1917 - February 28, 1943)
van Os, Hartog (June 12, 1899 - September 10, 1943)
Vijevoano, Mauritz (July 6, 1904 - December 8, 1943)
Weijel, Phillip (March 27, 1913 - March 8, 1943)
Worms, Levie (March 4, 1899 - November 15, 1942; buried at Bytom
Municipal Cemetery)

Additional information about the Jews buried in Bytom can be obtained from Moshe (Marian) Akselrad, the leader of Bytom's present-day Jewish community (Marian Akselrad, Kongregacia Zydowska, Ulica Jagielonska 19, m3-902, Bytom, Polska). In a conversation with Moshe Akselrad, I was told that there are now about 50 Jews living in Bytom, including six or seven children, a hopeful sign not common in Poland today. In 1962, there were 250 Jews in Bytom, and after the war the city even had a Talmud Torah. A small group of about twelve people prays on Shabbat and holiday mornings in Bytom's synagogue. In Bytom as in most of the Jewish communities of Poland, the weekly *parsha* is read on Shabbat from a *chumash* since there is no one capable of reading from the Torah itself. Intermarriage is widespread. Indeed, at the conclusion of our conversation, Moshe Akselrad inquired, with tears in his eyes, if I knew of a match for his son. When I suggested that the son, Tzvi (Henryk) Akselrad, should go to Israel or the United States to find a Jewish wife, his father protested that there weren't sufficient funds for such a journey. Tzvi Akselrad, age 36, six feet tall, weighing 175 pounds, was looking for a pretty girl. He declared that he would not object if she's religious, but she must be willing to live in Poland. His father, Moshe Akselrad, is married to a woman whose mother was married to a non-Jew. "I know that I'm Jewish," Tzvi told me, "but I want to know if my *yichus* is good enough to marry a Jewish girl."

Yet even as I was listening to Tzvi Akselrad's poignant la.aent, and even as I was reading the names on the tombstones in Bytom's Jewish cemetery, some good news reached me from Warsaw. Rabbi Joskowicz informed me that a Talmud Torah had been organized in Warsaw where Jewish children were learning about their faith from the *ba'al kriah* of the Warsaw synagogue, M. Shapira. In addition, a steady *minyan* had been formed with morning and evening services, including a class in *Mishnayot* taught by Rabbi Joskowicz between *mincha* and *maariv*. Rabbi Joskowicz also let me know that he delivers a talk every Shabbat morning before the *mussaf* services. The dry bones of the annihilated Polish Jewish community are beginning to stir; glimmers of life are returning in the field of devastation.

Top Left: Rabbi Weiss presentng Talith to Mr. Jakubowitz, President of Krakow Congregation in front of Isaak Reb Yekele's Synagogue

Top Right: Monument of the REMA at Krakow Cemetary

Left: Monument of Megaleh Amvicoth Rabbi Nosan Notel Shapiro at the Krakow Cemetary

Left: Prayer shawls displayed at Auschwitz

Right: Monument for 20,000 in Plaszow

Right: Polish lady recalls the destruction of the synagogue in Bochnia at rear

Chapter 12.
KRAKOW

I took out a volume of my *Mikraot Gedolot* during the three-hour train ride between Warsaw and Krakow, hoping, in this way, to attract the attention of a fellow Jew should one be traveling with me in the first-class compartment. I was disappointed. No one responded to my overtures. According to official counts, there are between five and seven thousand Jews living in Poland today, but unofficially it is believed that either there are at least twice as many, including numbers of people who are afraid to come forward and identify themselves as Jews, or half as many, because of the Jewish leadership's tendency to inflate the numbers.

If only we had in our day an advocate of our people of the caliber of the great Rabbi Levi Yitzchak of Berditchev. He would gaze over the devastation of the city of Krakow, the capital of Jewish Western Galicia, and cry out to God in a voice that would forever silence the strongest heavenly prosecutors who seek even more punishment for the Jewish people.

Before the war, Krakow had a population of 60,000 Jews, many of whom lived in a section of the city known as the Kazimierz. Of the three synagogues still standing in Krakow, the oldest, once known as "the fort", because Jews took refuge there in times of trouble, is now a museum.

The second synagogue, the Remu Synagogue on Ulica Sheroka or *Die Hoche Gass* (the High Street), is also known as *Bet Knesset*

Hechadash (the new synagogue). The synagogue was named in 1553 for the Rema, Rabbi Moshe Isserles, the great codifier. After being completely destroyed by fire, the synagogue was totally rebuilt. The Rema, as well as Rabbi Yom Tov Lippman Heller and Rabbi Nassan Nata Shapiro (known as the *Megaleh Amukot*), his wife and daughter, are all buried in the adjacent Jewish cemetery, the oldest in Krakow. A black fence encircles the grave of the Rema, and Jews come from all over on Lag B'Omer, the Rema's *yahrzeit*, to pray here. The traditional story connected with the Rema is that he lived 33 years, wrote 33 books, died on the thirty-third day of the Omer, and the rabbis who eulogized him listed 33 merits. The Rema died on Lag B'Omer, 1572, but, in fact, he lived 42 years rather than 33.

Legend has it that the Nazis spared the Remu Synagogue after being told that it was a holy place inhabited by the spirit of a holy man, and should they attempt to burn it down, they would fail in their mission. There is also another story about a wedding celebrated on Ulica Sheroka near the Remu Synagogue until late one Friday afternoon. The rabbi implored the guests to end the festivities lest they violate the Sabbath. When the guests went heedlessly on with their merry-making, the rabbi placed a curse on them. According to one account, they all died; another version has it that they were swallowed alive. In any case, after the Sabbath a fence was installed around the entire area. This fence remained standing until the Germans invaded Krakow and destroyed it.

The third synagogue still standing in Krakow is known as the Temple. Built in 1860, it is located on Ulica Miodowa 24. It is a huge building with a women's section in the balcony. A *mikvah* in the backyard is maintained by the Jewish community of Krakow. The Temple is now used only when many tourists are visiting the city. Otherwise, on Shabbat and holidays, services are held in the Remu Synagogue.

During my first return visit to Krakow almost thirty years ago, the Jewish community was profoundly agitated by a recent government decision to destroy the 400-year-old Remu Synagogue and cemetary to create a park in its place. Even more troubling, perhaps, was that the Jewish Communist leader, Dr. Boleslaw Drobner, approved of the government's decision, arguing that since a number of churches and Christian cemeteries were also being demolished, the destruction of the synagogue could not be regarded as a malevolent singling out of the Jews. However, Mr. Jacobowicz, one of the Jewish leaders, pointed out emphatically that the Remu Synagogue is not merely another place of worship; it is the symbol of one thousand years of Jewish life in Krakow.

At the time, the Remu Synagogue and the nearby cemetery were in a desperate state of neglect. Dogs and cats roamed freely, monuments were down, and the place had the appearance of a garbage dump. I suggested that a campaign be started to clean up the area and to restore the synagogue. As news spread of this campaign, thousands of letters came pouring into the Polish government protesting the destruction of the Jewish holy places. A restoration effort ensued, and today, the stones are upright and the site is maintained as a holy place. The gate to the cemetery and the door of the Remu Synagogue are opened and closed each morning and evening by the *shameste*, Chana Fogel, who took over her husband's duties when he died. An energetic woman who had been married three times, she also sees to it that the area is kept clean and she sets out a *kiddush* for the worshippers each Shabbat afternmoon; the *kiddush* is provided by the Joint Distribution Committee. The Remu Synagogue was remodeled as befits this monument to Krakow Jewish life and to the great Rabbi Moshe ben Yisroel Isserles.

Chapter 13.
THE REMA

The Rema, Rabbi Moshe ben Yisroel Isserles, was born in Krakow in the decade between 1520 and 1530. (*The Jewish Encyclopedia* of 1903 puts the year at 1520, while *The Encyclopaedia Judaica* suggests a birth year between 1525 and 1530.) According to some historians, the name Isserles is derived from the name of the Rema's father--Yisroel--called sometimes Yisrolik, Yisorelish, and possibly Isserlish. Other scholars explain that the family name was Isserlarz, which was shortened to Isserles.

Rabbi Yisroel, the father of the Rema, was an important figure in the Krakow Jewish community. A wealthy and charitable man, he traveled a great deal in his business, and is even mentioned as a *gaon*. His son addressed him as *Adoni Avi Mori Haparnass Hagadol* (My Master, My Father, My Teacher, the Great Leader). The Rema's early education was received in his father's house, where a great love of Torah and of Jewish scholarship was instilled in him. In his writings, the Rema refers to *halachic* decisions handed down by his father.

The Rema's secondary education was in Lublin under the renowned *gaon*, Rabbi Shalom Schachna, who followed the traditional pedagogical methods of Rabbi Yaakov Pollack, author of *Chilukim*. Under the guidance of Rabbi Schachna, young Moshe Isserles deepened his knowledge and understanding of Talmud and the commentaries, yet, at the same time, he maintained an appropriate modesty. This modesty, acquired during his Lublin years, is reflected in the foreword to his great work, *Torat Haolah*:. The Rema writes: *Hashem* the Creator of All has given me the great *zechus* to do what I have done although I do not possess any great wisdom or good deeds.'' The Rema continued his studies in Lublin until 1549, when he married Golda, Rabbi Schachna's daughter, and returned to Krakow immediately afterward.

Two years after the Rema's return to Krakow, he was overwhelmed by tragedy. The Great Plague swept through the city, taking with it many victims, including the Rema's mother on the tenth of Tevet, his twenty-year-old wife, and, sixteen days later, his grandmother. Nevertheless, the Rema continued his work as a *posek* and as *rosh yeshiva* to the hundreds of students who flocked to him.

In 1553, Rabbi Yisroel, the father of the Rema, built a wooden synagogue in memory of his wife. Some years later, the structure was consumed by fire, and Rabbi Yisroel replaced it with one made of stone. The building also housed the son's yeshiva. Today, a sign at the entrance informs the visitor that this is the ''*Bet Medrash Hechadash*,'' the new synagogue, to distinguish it from an older synagogue built 200 years earlier. Indeed, the synagogue is still referred to as the New Remu Synagogue. During the war, the Remu synagogue was used as living quarters, and in 1948 it was once again opened as a house of worship for the surviving Jews. To the right of the *aron kodesh* is a sign that says: ''We have a tradition that in this place the Rema stood as he poured out his prayers to *Hakodosh Baruch Hu*..'' A wooden board across the Rema's seat prevents visitors from using it. According to tradition, the Remu Synagogue possessed a Torah scroll written by the Rema himself, which the Krakow community guarded as its most sacred treasure. It was read from only on Yom Kippur and Simchat Torah. In 1940, when the Nazis came to Krakow, the Torah disappeared along with other holy items, and has never been found.

The story is told that after the death of his wife, Golda, the Rema approached his father-in-law, Rabbi Shalom Schachna, to ask for the hand of his second daughter. Rabbi Schachna refused, asserting that the Rema's eulogy at his first wife's funeral was so excellent, he must have composed it in advance. The Rema took as his second wife the daughter of Rabbi Mordechai Katz. They had two daughters and a son whom he mentions in responsa (*Sheaylot U'tshuvot*, Rema #122). His second daughter journeyed to Palestine after her marriage and settled in the city of Zefat.

The yeshiva of the Rema was known throughout Poland. The Rema, a wealthy man, provided for, as well as taught, hundreds of students, several of whom went on to do important work themselves. Among the Rema's most distinguished students was Rabbi Mordechai Yaffah, author of *Levushim*, who defended following the rulings of the Rema on the grounds that "there are no differences between the sages of Kaballah and religious philosophic scholars." Another Rema student was Rabbi David Ganz, author of *Tzemach David*, a history of the Jewish people.

When the Sephardic scholar, Rabbi Yosef Karo, published his famous *Shulchan Aruch* in 1564, the Rema felt that it needed to be amended to include various laws and customs pertaining to Ashkenazic Jews that had been agreed upon by the sages of France, Germany, and Poland. He therefore wrote a commentary, which he called *Mapah* (tablecloth), meant to be spread over the *Shulchan Aruch* (prepared table).

On the Friday morning that I arrived in Krakow, I went directly to the Jewish community building on Ulica Skavinska 2, on the corner of Ulica Krakowska. From there I was advised by Mr. Jacobowicz, the leader of the community, to come immediately to the Remu Synagogue, where he was addressing a group of 50 Viznitzer chassidim from Israel and America. The group graciously invited me to join them on an *erev Shabbat* visit to Auschwitz, an experience I shall never forget.

Chapter 14.
WITH THE VIZNITZER CHASSIDIM AT AUSCHWITZ

The fifty Viznitzer chassidim and their wives with whom I traveled from Krakow to Auschwitz were on a tour of Poland and Russia arranged by the Borough Park office of Rabbi Neiman, who, along with Reb Kalman, also served as the group's tour leader. As we rode to Auschwitz, our crowded bus passed the small town of Trzebinia, where the great *gaon*, Rav Dov Beresh Weidenfeld, had conducted a yeshiva before moving on to Israel to spread Torah to hundreds of students, and where Rabbi Benzion Halberstam, the father of the present-day Bobover Rebbe, Rabbi Shlomo Halberstam, lived and taught before the war. We also passed the town of Chrzanow, known, too, for its *gaonim* and *tzadikkim*, including Rabbi Dovid'l Krzanever, the son of the Sanzer Tzaddik, who along with his son, Moshe, as well as other sons, is buried in the Chrzanow cemetery. The Jewish cemetery in Chrzanow is kept in good order by a gentile who says he performs this service without payment in order to further Chrzanow's Jewish history. Today, there are no Jews or synagogues in either Trzebinia or Chrzanow.

As we made our way to Auschwitz, I mentioned to my hosts that I had grown up in the town of Oswiecim and they were eager to learn about Jewish life there, which I sought to portray in all its former beauty and vitality. Reb Kalman told me that the group was scheduled to move on to Russia that Sunday for visits to the graves of the Baal Shem Tov, of Rabbi Nachman of Bratslav in Uman, and other holy places.

Auschwitz was designated by the Nazis as the site for the final extermination of the Jewish people. In his autobiography, Rudolf Hoess quotes Himmler: "The Fuehrer has ordered that the Jewish question be solved once and for all, and that we, the SS are to implement that order. The existing extermination centers in the East are not in a position to carry out the large activities which are anticipated. I have therefore marked Auschwitz for this purpose, both because of its good position as regards communication and because the area can be easily isolated and camouflaged."

As soon as we arrived at Auschwitz, the Viznitzer men girded themselves in their *gartlech* and readied themselves for prayer. Our guide was John Monczak, a Pole who lived in Oswiecim. He spoke a Polish-accented English, which Reb Kalman translated into Yiddish for the visiting chassidim.

We entered all the blocks. A block is a building or unit in which the inmates were incarcerated, where they lived, suffered, and perished. On display in Block 4 is an urn filled with ashes that were once men, women, and children to represent the four million people who were murdered at Auschwitz. Also exhibited in Block 4 are models of gas chambers and crematoria, canisters of Zyklon B gas used to kill the victims, mountains of women's hair, shoes, valises, and one case filled with *talessim*.. When the chassidim came to the window behind which the *talessim* are displayed, they cried out, "*Vyinkom nikmat dam avadav hashafuch!*"" (May He avenge the spilled blood of his servants!) Their cries came from the very depths of their souls, and tears streamed down their faces.

Block 11 is known as the Death Block (*Bloc Smierci)*. No inmate came out alive from there. More than 20,000 prisoners were shot at close range against the Wall of Death in the yard of Block 11. Inside are dispalyed the punishment and torture devices used by the Germans on their victims.

Outside the main gate of the camp, near the gallows on which Rudolf Hoess was hanged on April 16, 1947, are the crematoria. When we reached the ovens, the chassidim lit candles and, with great emotion, began to recite *Tehilim*, concluding with the entire Psalm 119, "*Ashrei Temimei Derech*," recited sentence by sentence under the leadership of Reb Kalman. Afterward, everyone recited *Kaddish* together. The cries of the chassidim went up to the very heart of heaven. As for the Poles in charge of Auschwitz, however, they seem deaf to the fact that the majority of those who were killed there were Jews, for there is only scant and then only grudging reference to the millions of Jews who perished at Auschwitz-Birkenau.

When we returned to Krakow late that Friday afternoon, I was struck with admiration over the preparations Rabbi Neiman had managed to make for Shabbat. An *airuvei chatzerot* was put up in the Forum Hotel where the chassidim were based to permit them to carry, and there was even a *cholent* on the fire. Rabbi Neiman generously invited me to join them for the Shabbat meals, but because I wanted to be closer to the Remu Synagogue, I bid my new friends farewell, though I was not allowed to return to my hotel to make my preparations for Shabbat until I was laden with enough food and supplies for all the meals.

Chapter 15.
SHABBAT IN KRAKOW

When I served as *baal tefila* in the Remu Synagogue and delivered a talk from the same *bimah* on which the great *gaon* and scholar, Rabbi Moshe ben Yisroel Isserles, prayed and taught the *Shulchan Aruch* and *Mapah* I had been studying so many years, a rare feeling of elevation and transcendence overwhelmed me. Only a few times in my life had I ever been overcome by such a sense of exhiliration. When I entered the Ibn Ezra Synagogue in Egypt, for instance, and a sign informed me that "Here stood Moses and spread his hands to *Hashem* to stop the plague," I was profoundly moved by my proximity to such greatness and I uttered a heartfelt prayer. In the Sinai Desert, treading the very soil the children of Israel had wandered for forty years, I felt myself again to be exquisitely uplifted. And some years ago, when I was invited to officiate for the High Holidays in the Ari Synagogue in Zefat and I--*ani hakatan,* Moshe ben David--stood where the incomparable Ari had stood, I felt my spirit soaring, just as I felt myself borne aloft once again as I stood at the *bimah* in Krakow in the synagogue of the great Rema.

That Friday night, when I entered the Remu Synagogue, there were only seven men gathered. The two *gabbaim* were waiting for three more people to wander in. When they finally arrived, I was asked to lead the services. I noticed immediately several strange things. While reciting *Kaddish* and *Kedusha,* for example, there was complete silence from the congregation. Also, during *Shmoneh Esreh* and *Kedusha*, most of the assembled were sitting. At the end of the service, one man rose and recited *Kaddish* with a Polish accent. When I asked Mr. Beck, one of the *gabbaim*, why I had heard no Amen, or any other response from the congregation, he answered with embarrassment that some of those assembled were either not Jewish or did not know how to read. I realized then that I had officiated over a congregation that had no *minyan* of Jews. Mr. Beck told me they were grateful if anyone came to the synagogue, and that they took the Torah out only when there was someone present who could read it.

I returned to my hotel room, saddened once again at how drastically the Polish Jewish community had been reduced. When I returned to the synagogue the next day at the scheduled hour, there was still no *minyan*. At nine-thirty, the tenth man walked in, and again I conducted the service with little cooperation from the congregation. In my sermon, I sought to revive the *atzmaot yevaishot*, the dry bones, and to instill some spirit in the hearts of the assembled. Indeed, I wondered, *Hatichyena haatzmaot haeleh* ? Will these bones ever live again?

During the *kiddush* I learned from Mr. Beck that non-Jews come to the services in order to partake of the refreshments afterward. Mr. Beck, whose wife had died ten years earlier and who now lived with his ninety-year-old mother, told me that most of the Jewish men have gentile wives. In Poland today, one does not need a Jewish wife in order to serve as *chazzan*. Mr. Beck officiates occasionally, as does another *gabbai*, Mr. Stein, a former major in the Polish army and now in the reserves. A third *gabbai*, Mr. White, has a daughter by his Polish wife. Though from all appearances Mr. White seems to be earning a good living, he, like all the others, including Mr. Beck, a peddler of used clothes, had his hand out. They were all anxious to receive some of the clothing that I announced I would be distributing.

For the *Mussaf* service we were joined by about one hundred boys and girls from the Bnei Akiva in Israel, who had made the trip to Poland with a staff of youth leaders in order to learn about their Jewish past. The Remu Synagogue, with an estimated capacity for about fifty to sixty people, was crowded that day. The *gabbai* called people up during the reading of the Torah, but who could be sure that all of them were Jewish? I was given *Maftir*, and I could not help but think that if Ezra the Scribe were present at these services, he would surely repeat the speech he gave to the Jews returning from the Babylonian exile, urging them to send away their non-Jewish wives. Here in the devastation that was once Jewish Krakow, in the Remu Synagogue, would such words from Ezra fall on deaf ears?

My attention was drawn to one of the worshippers in the synagogue that day who appeared to be a chassidic Jew with a black hat and black coat, but he was not wearing a *tallit*. When he attempted to put one on, a *gabbai* approached and removed it from his back. Later I learned that this man was not a Jew. His name is Yusef Misholek, and he has been coming to the Remu Synagogue every Saturday morning for the past six years. He has not missed a single Sabbath. He never says a word during the services, but in private he has confided that he wants to move to Israel and become a rabbi. Occasionally, he attempts to sit at the eastern wall, near the chair traditionally held to be the one in which the Rema himself sat, but a *gabbai* always approaches and asks him to move to the rear.

The *gabbaim*, afraid of the authorities, cannot risk asking Misholek to leave. Misholek reminded me of the young Communist I had seen sitting at the entrance to the Moscow synagogue every Saturday morning, writing down the names of all those who came and went. Nobody knows who Misholek is. For me, the strange Misholek and the frightened way in which the *gabbaim* felt constrained to tolerate his disturbing presence, was only one more sad reminder of the bitter decline of what was once the flourishing Jewish community of Krakow.

On that Shabbat afternoon as I walked into the remodelled Synagogue of Isaac B'Reb Yekeles in Krakow, my guide asked me "Do you know why this beautiful Shul is called by that name? I'll tell you" he said, without my responding to his question.

Isaac the son of Reb Yekele lived in Krakow several hundred years ago. He was a very poor man and prayed to Hashem to make him rich, so that he might be able to perform many mitzvot. Night after night he dreamt that he should go to the city of Prague. There he was to dig under the government bridge where he would find a great treasure. When his dream kept reoccurring, he decided to save enough money for his journey to Prague.

As soon as he reached the city of Prague, he immediately went to the bridge. There he noticed soldiers guarding the bridge. He waited several days, hoping the soldiers would leave the area. Day after day and even at night he circled around the bridge, but the soldiers did not leave.

One day the head of the guards noticed Isaac near the bridge and asked what he was doing there. Reb Isaac decided to tell him about his dream he had in Krakow and that this was the reason he was there. Upon hearing this the guard laughed and said "Dreams are false, only fools believe in dreams. If I would be the fool you are, I too would travel to a far off land, for I also had a dream that a man came to me and told me to go to the city of Krakow and start digging in the home of a Jew called Isaac Yekeles. There under his over I would find a great treasure.'' ''Just imagine'' the guard continued, ''I heard that in the city of Krakow there are tens of thousands of Jews and probably half of them are named Yekele, I would have to break up all Jewish homes in order to find my dream treasure.''

Upon hearing this, Reb Isaac returned to the hotel, packed his bags and went back to Krakow. There he dug under his stove and indeed found much gold and became a very rich man. He gave a great deal of charity to the poor and needy and built a beautiful Synagogue in Krakow, and named it The Isaac B'Reb Yekeles Shul.

Chapter 16.
PLASZOW

Before departing Krakow on a sunny Sunday morning, I was handed a list of local Jews still seeking lost friends and relatives. More than five decades have passed since the devastating events occurred that ripped families and communities apart, yet these Krakow Jews still nurture the hope of reuniting with lost loved ones. Here are their names and addresses:

Barbaz, Eliaz, Ulica Katarzyny 4/5
Beck, Yakub, Ulica Reytana 12/11
Broch, Erwin, Ulica Sienna 12/13
Fogel, Chana, Ulica Dietla 49/21
Gringrass, Yozef, Ulica Mala 5/12
Lempel, Leon, Ulica Stachowicza Azory 25/101
Lesniakowski, Yosef, Ulica Reymonta 4/120
Lieban, Yan, Ulica Gregorzecka 45/32
Nas, Henryk, Ulica Lubiez 40/11
Rand, Yulian, Ulica Zwierzyniecka 17/25
Reiner, Yosef, Ulica Augustyanska 4/13
Szmer, Fryda, Ulica Miodawa 55/1
Sztein, Wladzimierz, Ulica Osna Wzgorach 3/4
Szyrynska, Pologia, Ulica 18 Stycznia 92/66
Yakubowicz, Herman, Ulica Stawkowska 30/2
Yam, Mauryey, Ulica Bochenska 8/37
Zawada, Fryderyka, Ulica Lezcka 2/63
Zdzislaw, Yekiel, Ulica Boch Stalingradu 97/17

My companion for the fifteen minute ride from Krakow to Plaszow was Yossel Berger, a former inmate of the concentration camp that had been situated there. Plaszow is not a town, and hardly even a village. No houses are visible. It sits on the highway leading to Wieliczka, where the great salt mines operate. Yossel and I walked up the Plaszow hill to the *pomnik* (monument) bearing an inscription that this was the site of a forced labor camp where tens of thousands of people were killed, though no specific mention is made of the Jews who constituted the majority of the camp's victims. The Nazis operated this camp from June, 1942 and it was dismantled in January 1945.

At first, the camp was occupied by the Jews of Krakow and its environs. In September 1942, 2,000 Jews were delivered to Plaszow from the Tarnow ghetto. In April 1943, after the Krakow ghetto was disbanded, the Nazis sent 6,000 Jews to Plaszow. Approximately 1,500 Jews, mostly women, were brought from Hungary to Plaszow in January 1944. At one time, there were over 20,000 inmates in the camp. They were assigned to hard labor at factories where they worked with metal, glass, and stone, and they even manufactured clothing for German companies. In March 1944, many of the Jewish inmates were transported to Auschwitz while others were sent to Mathausen, Stuthoff, and Flossenberg. Just before the war ended, Jewish inmates were ordered to burn 9,000 bodies that were removed from eleven mass graves. When the Russians liberated Plaszow, they found only 600 inmates in the camp, which was disbanded soon after. In 1946, the SS commander of the Plaszow camp, Amon Gat, was sentenced to death.

Yossel Berger told me that Polish peasants claim they can still hear, to this day, the cries of tormented Jews that issued from the Plaszow camp. The peasants believe that the murdered men, women, and children still gather together in the night to weep over their fate. For that reason, Berger said, the Plaszow area is now nearly deserted. The younger Poles have moved away, and the older inhabitants are afraid to step out of their homes at night.

Refusing to believe the peasants' stories, Berger told me that he decided to spend a night in a Plaszow home. ''In the darkness of the night,'' Berger recalled, ''I heard terrible sounds of bitter crying from the camp. Please believe me. I heard the cries of men, women, and children. As the night advanced, the cries became louder. In particular, I heard the cries of the children and I knew that they were Jewish children. When the sun came up, the weeping subsided. I can never forget what I heard. Even now, in my own home, the cries of my fellow Jews remain in my ears.''

Berger also told of a young SS officer who fell in love with a beautiful Jewish woman at Plaszow. He courted her and lived with her, and he provided her with sufficient food and clothing. When, after six months, the woman broke her ankle, her lover attended to her needs. But then, when he sensed that his illicit liaison had been detected by his fellow officers, the SS man shot his mistress to death at close range.

Inmates who sought to escape from Plaszow, Berger told me, were whipped publicly by Ukrainian guards at the orders of the camp commander, Amon Gat. A minimum of fifty lashes were administered upon their naked bodies, and the victims were forced to count each lash out loud. Bloody and faint, if they lost count, the punishment was started again from the beginning. Those who passed out were revived with cold water, and the whipping continued.

That night, I dreamed I saw thousands of skeletons, their arms outstretched, crying for help. When I awoke with great relief in the morning, I recited the *Modeh Ani* with extra fervor, deeply grateful to God for restoring my soul to my body. Before leaving Plaszow, I recited a *Molei* at the monument for the victims of this terrible place, victims whose heartrending cries still pierce the serenity of the night.

Chapter 17.
WIELICZKA

About a twenty minute ride from Plaszow is the town of Wieliczka, where my grandparents had a business which was later taken over by my parents. I vividly remember how my father and my older brother would travel the fifty kilometers to Wieliczka from our home in Oswiecim. In Wieliczka, too, I hoped to find the cemetery and grave where my grandmother Temme is buried.

My grandfather, Reb Anschel, and his wife Temme lived for a time in Wieliczka. Before coming to Wieliczka, Reb Anschel was a *meshamesh bakodesh* to the Sanzer Rebbe, Rabbi Chaim Halberstam, and then, until 1899, he served as the *gabbai* to the Sanzer's son, Rabbi Yechezkel Shragai Halberstam. When Rabbi Yechezkel passed away in 1899, my grandparents moved to Wieliczka, where my grandmother Temme practiced as a licensed midwife. To this day I still meet people who tell me that they were brought into this world by my grandmother Temme.

Once known for its salt mines, Wieliczka is now a city where a visitor can still find embedded in the pavement Jewish tombstones that the Nazis used to repair sidewalks. Many of these were dug up and brought back to the cemetery. "If you are looking for Jews," the officer at the police station curtly informed me, "there aren't any. This town, thank God, is *Judenrein*. As for dead Jews, they're everywhere." He directed my driver to the cemetery.

The cemetery is an overgrown field high on top of the mountain. No sign or wall demarcates it. How could a funeral procession ever make its way to this mountain top? I wondered. Ninety-five percent of the tombstones are down. A *pomnik* with a plaque inscribed with the names of ten murdered Wieliczka Jews, stands in the cemetery, erected there by Jews returning from Russia after the war.

During my last visit to Wieliczka three decades ago, I searched for the few remaining Jews. Inquiring at the police station, where about thirty clerks sat at desks deeply engrossed in their bureaucratic duties, I asked, "Are there any Jews in Wieliczka?" At the mention of the word *Zhydy* (Jews), thirty heads looked up. "*Zhydy?* Here in Wieliczka? *Niema Zhydy!* (No Jews!)"

As I turned to leave, I heard a voice from the back. A young girl was politely asking me to wait. She knew of one family, she said, an elderly, ailing couple, the Schnurs, who lived not far from the police station.

The Schnurs lived in a large, nicely furnished apartment that clearly, at one time, had been a prosperous residence. They had inherited a flourishing family business, and when they married they took in a young Polish maid from nearby Bochnia who remained to help them raise their children.

When the Nazis entered Wieliczka and took over the salt mines and businesses, the Schnur children, now grown, urged their parents to flee with them from Poland. Disguised in Polish army uniforms, the children made their way to Eastern Galicia through the Russian border. The parents, however, remained in Wieliczka.

As the Jews of Wieliczka were rounded up in the marketplace to be transported to forced labor camps, it seemed to the Schnurs that they were doomed. It was then that their Polish maid saved them, taking them to her parents' home in Bochnia where she hid them in a dry well about two meters wide and five meters deep. This is where they remained until the war ended.

Because the vacated Jewish apartments were routinely taken over by the Poles, the Schnurs suggested that their Polish maid reside there in their absence. Every day, however, the maid journeyed to Bochnia to bring food and necessities to the Schnurs. During those dark days, feeling their existence to be hopeless and depressing, the Schnurs were often tempted to emerge from hiding and give up. It was only the maid's encouragement and devotion that convinced them to persevere.

Their return to their apartment in Wieliczka was hardly greeted with enthusiasm by their Polish neighbors, but their maid welcomed them home and continued to serve them. When I visited them for the first time, the Schnurs were ill and bed-ridden, but still they were being taken care of by their devoted maid.

Now, thirty years later, in the Jewish cemetery of Wieliczka, I was once again visiting the Schnurs. Their tombstones stood side by side. Nearby was the grave of their saintly maid, a righteous gentile, faithful in death as she had been in life.

Chapter 18.
THE WATCHMAKER AND THE RABBI'S SON
OF WIELICZKA

The young girl at the Wieliczka police station who, thirty years ago, had directed me to the Schnurs also told me of a watchmaker from Tchernovitz, Romania, who had arrived in town after the war. I found this watchmaker in his repair shop in the marketplace, sitting over his work with a loupe wedged into one eye. Arrayed behind him was a display of watches and instruments. Extending my hand to him, I greeted him warmly. "*Shalom aleichem*," I said. The watchmaker recoiled, leaving my hand dangling in midair. "*Co pan chce?*" (What do you want?) he cried.

I explained to the watchmaker that I was an American rabbi searching for Jews. "You have the wrong address. I am a Pole and this is a Polish watchmaker's shop." "But a policewoman gave me your name and address and told me you were a Jew," I countered. His face turned white. "They have surely made a mistake. How can they say such a thing? They see me in church every Sunday. I'm the first to kneel when the priest passes in his carriage ringing his bell. Obviously, this is a mistake."

At this point, I decided to try another approach. Pleading that my Polish is somewhat weak, I asked if we might continue our conversation in German. He repeated his story, then, in a German so Yiddishized as to immediately identify him as a Jew, one of the "Marranos" of the Polish exile, a Marrano not because of Polish or church law, but out of sheer fright, loneliness, and despair.

"Have no fear," I consoled him. "I've only come to help. By now you must understand that you can't hide your identity. You are a Jew. You look like a Jew. Everyone knows you're a Jew." Yet despite all this, he still refused to admit it. But when I inquired if there were any other Jews in town, he replied in a more forthcoming way, mentioning the Schnurs, the Zellners, and a Mrs. Sobel who operated a fruit store in the *Rynek* (marketplace). As I left his shop, I reflected upon the pathetic destiny that had overtaken this sad watchmaker, his futile attempt to escape an identity that however adamantly he denied it, the gentiles would never allow him to forget.

Mrs. Sobel lived in back of her fruit store in the upper marketplace with her partner, another widow. To my relief, she replied to my "*Shalom aleichem*" with a hearty "*aleichem shalom*" in a rich Galician Yiddish. I felt absolutely at home when she told me that my grandmother Temme was the midwife who had delivered her, and she even remembered where my grandparents had lived. She offered to take me on a tour of the formerly Jewish sections of Wieliczka, and while her partner minded the shop, we walked around the town. I saw my grandparents' house, the store they had once operated, and also the *Plasky Kamien*, a town landmark, a natural rock formation that had been a popular meeting place for the local citizenry.

Mrs. Sobel also led me to many empty areas that had once contained synagogues and yeshivot, and were now identified as such with plaques. She had been incarcerated in the Plaszow concentration camp from the beginning of the war until nearly the end, Mrs. Sobel told me. When she discovered that the Nazis were planning to transport the inmates to Auschwitz for eventual annihilation, Mrs. Sobel began to plan her escape. As Plaszow was being transformed from a forced labor camp to an extermination center, a fence was erected around it. Mrs. Sobel bribed one of the SS guards, jumped the fence, and managed to survive. "Believe me, I don't know how I did it! Only *Eliyahu Hanavi* could have carried me over that fence!"

We returned to the store and I watched as customers came and went. We reminisced about the old days in this unique town. Suddenly, the door opened and in strode a young gentile, a giant of a man, who had to stoop over almost double in order to make his way into the shop. Husky, even obese, he resembled a Slavic wrestler, though, incongruously, his facial features were rather delicate. Mrs. Sobel greeted him politely, as she did all her customers. "*Dzien dobry, Pan*

Yuzek!" ("Good day, Mr. Yuzek.") When there was no response, she turned to him again. "Yuzek," she said, "I want you to meet an important person. This is a rabbi from America!"

Yuzek walked over to me, all seven feet six inches of him, placed his massive hands on my lapels, lifted me from the ground, and shook me like a *lulav*, all the while spewing filthy curses against the Jews. Naturally, I was alarmed. When he finished with me, he set me back down on the ground, bought some fruits and vegetables, and still mumbling imprecations against the Jews, left the store. "Mrs. Sobel," I said, "I have a wife and children. *Hut rachmonos*! Have pity! Why did you do this to me?"

"Rabbi Weiss," said Mrs. Sobel, "I simply wanted to introduce you to the son of the rabbi of Wieliczka. Yuzek is no *goy*. He's a Jew, the son of the former rabbi of the town, Rabbi Pinchas Halberstam. His face is identical to that of the late rabbi, and the Polish family that had raised him admits he's not their son. They claim to have found the boy in the streets of the town, and since no one would tell them to whom the child belonged, the Poles took him in and raised him as their own."

According to the Jewish survivors of Wieliczka, the rabbi's wife had placed her child near a Polish house when the Nazis ordered the rounding up of the Jewish citizens in the marketplace. A virulently anti-Semitic Polish family named Checha took in the boy, raised him as a Christian, and instilled in him a deep hatred of the Jews. A Jewish doctor who had once treated Yuzek in the hospital disclosed that the boy had been circumcised. Poles never circumcised their children.

When I returned to Wieliczka thirty years after my first visit, I inquired about Yuzek Checha. His Polish parents had died, I was told, and he still lived in their home, still a committed Jew-hater. Luckily, there are no Jews left in Wieliczka against whom the giant Yuzek could direct his hatred, though when it come to to anti-Semitism, the absence of Jews, it seems, has never been a significant impediment.

Chapter 19.
THE BRIDGE IN KRAKOW--AN INTERLUDE

When I returned from Wieliczka to Krakow, tired and depressed, I sat down near the bridge that spans the Vistula River and wept over all the desolation I had witnessed. I wept as our ancestors had wept by the waters of Babylon two and one half millennia ago over the destruction of our Temple and our exile from the Holy Land. I wept as I remembered the Poland before the catastrophe of the war. Like the prophet Jeremiah who had witnessed the services in the Holy Temple, I, a simple man, Moshe the son of David, also grieved. Like Jeremiah, I asked: "*Aicha yashva badad ha'ir rabati am, hayta k'almanah?*" "How does the city sit solitary, like a widow, that once was so full of people?" The great cities of Poland--Warsaw, Krakow, Lodz, Lublin, Tarnow, Bialystok, even my hometown of Oswiecim--where Jewish life had once flourished and thrived, were now desolate, forsaken like childless widows.

Although Poland had never been without anti-Semitism, Jewish life, and, in particular, the Torah way of life, had flourished there. Jews built a great society of distinguished rabbis, scholars, and righteous men. Every town had its synagogues, its yeshivot, its centers of learning, its old age homes, its community centers providing all the necessary religious services. Now there was nothing.

Today, only seven synagogues remain in all of Poland. Services, held only on the Sabbath and holidays, are attended by hardly more than a minimum quorum. No one is capable of reading the Torah from the scroll. There, by the bridge spanning the Vistula River, I wept as I remembered the Poland that once was and is no more.

And while Poland is now undergoing profound changes, Jewish
Poland is finished. Who can imagine Poland without the Sabbath as I
once knew it? It was a day of rest not only for human beings but for all
creation. The *Shabbat* radiance filled the home, the street, the entire
neighborhood. Polish Jews prayed three times a day, but never as
ardently as they did on Shabbat. The chassidim sang in their *shtiblach*;
the *mitnagdim* prayed in the *bet medrash*; the modern Jews held services
in their synagogues and temples. There were early worshippers and late
worshippers. Some would not start their prayers until they learned a
section of Talmud. Chassidim immersed themselves in the *mikvah*
before beginning Sabbath prayers. Never was Jewish life so rich and
vibrant.

With the destruction of Polish Jewry, a great part of the Jewish soul
has been lost. If one thousand years of Jewish life could be so brutally
and swiftly annihilated, how could Jews feel utterly safe anywhere? Yet
in our day we have Israel, and despite everything, the Jewish people live.
"My vengeance is life," wrote the survivor, Susan Felix, in a poem
once given to me by Dorothy Jacobs of Millbrae, California:

> My vengeance is to live
> Take heed makers of death and sorrow.
> Brutalizers of life--
> I will pour sunshine into the world
> Bring air and light to stifling places
> Open windows and doors,
> Sing in the streets and dance in the fields.
> My vengeance is life.

Rising from my place of sorrow beside the Vistula River, I was
approached by an elderly man who had been sitting nearby and
observing me. "I noticed you're wearing a *kappel* on your head," he
said, "and I saw tears streaming from your eyes. Are you all right?"

"I'm fine," I replied.

"My best friends were Jews who wore *kappels* like yours. As a
matter of fact, I used to visit them on Fridays and Saturdays to turn their
lights on and off and to watch the *cholent* on the fire so that it wouldn't
burn. I loved the *challah* they gave me every week. Jews were my best
friends."

"Do you miss them?" I asked.

"I miss their *challah* and their *cholent.*," he said. "I was their
Shabbos goy." He then told me that he is still living in the home that
he had expropriated after its Jewish owners had been taken away by the
Nazis.

"What if this family of Jews were to return and reclaim their home?" I inquired.

He jumped at this. "Do you remember what happened at Kielce when the Jews returned and tried to reclaim their homes?" he asked ominously. He did not need to say another word. I now understood what kind of man this was with whom I was speaking.

When the Jews returned to Kielce after the war they were massacred by the Poles who had taken over their homes and all their possessions. The man with whom I was conversing missed the Jewish *challah* and *cholent*t; he did not miss the Jewish people. Those ubiquitous gentiles I had observed in the synagogues also come not out of love for the Jewish people, but for a slice of Jewish *challah* and a bowl of Jewish *cholent*.

Chapter 20.
BOCHNIA

As we were about to enter the taxi for a visit to the town of Bochnia, my guide, Yossel Berger, bent over, picked up some potato peelings from the ground, and stuffed them into his pocket. When he noticed that I had observed his actions, he smiled in a sad and embarrassed way, explaining that at the age of eight, when the Nazis invaded his town, he had been forced to scavenge for food through the garbage heaps. To this day, Yossel said, he is still not free of the anxiety that he will go hungry, and when he sees a potato or its peelings in the gutter, he cannot resist pocketing them. As Yossel related this pathetic tale to me, he flung the potato peelings out of the window of the moving car.

In his usual thorough fashion, Yossel briefed me during our journey to Bochnia on the details about Wieliczka that he had not yet covered and also provided me with background information about the town of Bochnia where we would soon arrive. When the Germans entered Wieliczka on September 8, 1939, Yossel told me, the Jewish population was 1,300, which was increased over the ensuing years by forced relocations from nearby communities. On August 27, 1942, 8,000 Jews were deported from the Wieliczka ghetto to the Belzec concentration camp, 500 Jews were sent to forced labor at Salowa-Wola, and 200 were transported to Plaszow.

Bochnia, like Wieliczka, is a small town belonging to the province of Krakow. From 1939-1945, Bochnia was known as Salzberg (Salt Mountain) because of its rock salt deposits, while Wieliczka was known for its salt mines. Jews had been living in Bochnia since 1555, and for centuries they were salt miners as well as marketers and contractors for the exportation of rock salt. The legendary Saul Wohl, the famous Jewish "King for a Day," had also supposedly been involved in the production of salt and rock salt in these two towns.

In 1605, a Jewish miner who had been caught stealing salt was tortured and executed, resulting in the expulsion of the Jews of Bochnia and the declaration of the town as "*de non tolerandes Judaeis.*" The Jewish population of Bochnia scattered to nearby locations, including the capital, Krakow. In 1662, Jews were granted permission to return to Bochnia and to resume their old occupations--mining and exporting rock salt.

At the beginning of the Second World War, there were 3,500 Jews in Bochnia, and the town was flourishing with rabbis and teachers, synagogues and places of learning. The Germans entered Bochnia on September 3, 1939, changing its name to Salzberg, and instituting their reign of terror. Early in 1940, the invaders ordered the leaders of the Jewish community to submit a *Kontribution* of three million zlotys (about $600,000) to the Nazi occupation.

In 1942, a ghetto was established for the Jews of Bochnia and the surrounding areas. In August, 1942, an *Aktion* was carried out by police units from Krakow, who gathered all the Jews in the marketplace and summarily executed 600 of them. They also deported 2,000 for extermination at Belzec. In November, another *Aktion* resulted in the immediate killing of seventy Jews and the deportation of 500 more to Belzec. After this, the ghetto was divided into two parts: Ghetto A became a forced labor camp, and Ghetto B, a concentration camp. By the end of 1942, the Bochnia ghetto was officially liquidated. The Jews of Ghetto A were deported to the Szebnia camp, where very few survived. The Ghetto B Jews were sent to Auschwitz. After the war, no Jews returned to Bochnia.

"*Niema Zhydy!*" (No Jews) was the familiar refrain that I heard at the Bochnia police station when I entered the town. For some unfathomable reason, it was uttered a bit more politely than usual. It did not seem to have buried within it the implicit message that not only were there no Jews in Bochnia, but no Jews were wanted.

I searched for the Jewish cemetery of Bochnia, but nobody could tell me where it was located. I searched for a plaque to indicate that once there had been Jewish life here, but there was no commemoration of any sort. In the neighboring village of Klasna I again sought evidence of the

Jewish existence that had been there. My efforts were in vain. We continued on our way to Dabrowa where many Jews had lived before the war. On my last visit to this town three decades earlier, there were twenty Jews. Now there was none.

As we drove to Dabrowa, my guide, Yossel Berger, recalled the first selection by the Nazis in the the marketplace of his town. Yossel's father, a community leader and fluent in German, stepped forward and was struck and knocked unconscious by a Nazi soldier wielding a rubber club. Later Yossel learned that this was because his father had refused to shave off his beard and sidelocks. The women and children, Yossel among them, were herded into the dark synagogue, all the while being ordered by the Germans to hand over their jewelry and valuables. Yossel knew of a good hiding place inside the synagogue, where he remained until the selection was over.

Recalling all this as we traveled on the road to Dabrowa, tears streamed down Yossel Berger's face. The passage of the years had done nothing to diminish the humiliation and the loss.

Chapter 21.
ZABNO AND DABROWA

The straight highway from Krakow to the Russian border passes through many towns and villages: Wieliczka, Bochnia, Tarnow, Rzeszow, and Przemysl. Before entering Tarnow, we turned left in the direction of Zabno and Dabrowa. As we traveled, my guide, Yossel Berger, talked ceaselessly. The bitterness welled up in him as he recalled not only how Polish Jewry had been annihilated during the war, but how the survivors had been treated in the subsequent years. Jews returning from the camps to reclaim their homes and businesses were attacked, beaten, and even murdered by Polish mobs in Kielce, Sanz, and other cities and towns. And despite the half-hearted attempts of the post-War Communist regime to suppress the anti-Semitism so deeply rooted in the Polish population, following the 1967 Six Day War, anti-Semitism was given a new and virulent legitimacy in the form of anti-Zionism. Stigmatizing Jews as disloyal Polish citizens, Gomulka openly invited them to emigrate to Israel. Of course, many Jews who regarded themselves as loyal Polish citizens as well as loyal communists refused to leave their country, and they were subjected to a whole range of abuse and discrimination.

During my last visit to Zabno, a small town near Dabrowa, I found only one remaining Jew, and a cemetery half destroyed and buried over. I did manage to find one tombstone inscribed with the name of the Zabner Rebbe, Rabbi Unger, the father of the famous Yiddish writer, Menashe Unger. Today, there is not a single Jew left in Zabno.

In Dabrowa, the huge synagogue I had visited thirty years earlier was still standing, though I was unable to find anyone who could open its doors. Today, only one Jew remains in Dabrowa, Shmuel Roth, residing at Ulica Dashinskiego 8. But during my earlier visit, Dabrowa was extraordinary among Polish towns in that twenty Jews still lived there, a huge number by post-War standards, a veritable *kehila* such as might be found in one of the larger cities.

Of the twenty Jews I had located in Dabrowa during my first visit, almost one-third did not regard themselves to be full-fledged members of the faith. Most did not know how to read or write Hebrew. They knew little or nothing about the movement to resettle Israel. The great edifice that had once been the town's central synagogue bore no sign or marking of its former status as a place of worship.

In order to enter the synagogue, a visitor required the permission of the police. The man whom the magistrate sent along with me carried a bag containing the gigantic key to the synagogue. Two hands were needed to manipulate the key in the lock. When we entered the synagogue, my companion put a yarmulke on his head because, as he told me, his "mother and father had Jewish blood." A member of the Communist party, his name was Yuzek Adler, and he was in charge of the synagogue.

The synagogue was huge and cavernous, capable of holding two or three thousand worshippers. Our footsteps echoed in its hollow depths. The walls were charred. The benches were covered with dust and cobwebs. The curtain of the holy ark was red, with a black border. Most of the windows were broken, and the wind howled through the building. The ark's curtain fluttered in the wind. The twelve *mazalot*, depicting the signs for each month of the year, could still be discerned on the walls. The *mazal*, "*tleh*," the little sheep for the month of Nissan, looked down upon us with what seemed to be fear and sorrow, as though she were carrying upon her back the destruction of her entire flock. All the other sheep were missing. On the ceiling was depicted the *Kinor Dovid*, the harp of David, and remnants of a painting of the grave of Mother Rachel and the Tower of David. I thought of Rabbi Mordechai David'l of Dabrowa, who had once presided as the spiritual leader of this august place of worship.

With trembling steps I followed Yuzek from the entrance on the west to the ark at the east. When I drew back the curtain I saw the black charred parchment remains of the Torah scroll. Yuzek himself had never looked inside the ark in all his years of carrying the key.

Noticing my fright, Yuzek asked me what I had seen. I thought of the martyr, Rabbi Chanina ben Teradyon, who had been wrapped in the Torah scroll as he was burned by the Romans. "What do you see?" his students asked their martyred rabbi. I see "*gevilin nisrafim v'otiyot porchot ba'avir*"; "I see parchment burning and the letters hovering in the air." In the great synagogue of Dabrowa, the letters of the Torah were in the air.

"Can you read this?" I asked Yuzek, as I unrolled one of the parchment scrolls. When he answered that he could not, I decided to read for him. The scroll opened to the chapter *in Pinchas*, to the section dealing with the laws of inheritance: "If a man dies and has no son, the inheritance passes to his daughter. If there is no daughter, it goes to the brothers. And if he has no brothers, the inheritance goes to the father's brother. And if there is no brother, then the inheritance goes to the kinsman next to him in the family."

Yuzek understood. He, too, possessed Jewish blood. The inheritance should go to him. Since he was one of the very few who had survived of the generation that had perished, he, by right, should be the heir. "I must go back to the magistrate," Yuzek said, as he watched me recite the prayer, *Uvenucho Yomar*.

As we left the synagogue, Yossel Berger said to me bitterly, "What happened in the synagogue should remind you Jews in America and in Israel that there are no heirs left in Poland. You are the heirs of the one thousand years of Polish Jewish history."

Chapter 22.
TARNOW

A popular folk song tells of a shepherd who searches everywhere for his lost flock, stopping all the people he meets to inquire if they had seen his sheep. The answer, of course, is no. The *chazzan* of Tarnow whom I had once met was such a shepherd. From his tiny apartment in the Jewish community building on Ulica Goldhamera he devoted himself to finding the lost Jews of Tarnow. Only the lucky ones could be found in the scattered graves of the city. The rest were bones and ashes.

Chazzan Michal Gutter-Bergstein, who, at one time, was in charge of all community activities, was, when I met him, mainly involved in assisting people who desired to visit the graves of their loved ones. Any individual wishing to commemorate a *yahrzeit* would contact Chazzan Gutter-Bergstein, and together they would visit the gravesite where the *chazzan* would recite a *Molei* and a *kaddish*. Whenever a community decided to erect a public memorial for a mass grave of the kind that can still be found all over Poland, Chazzan Gutter-Bergstein was summoned to conduct the service. He was extremely popular and well-regarded among the Jews in the Krakow-Tarnow district. The first time I met Chazzan Gutter-Bergstein was at a memorial ceremony held annually at the mass grave of 800 children who were killed by the Nazis in a single day. After the *Chazzan* spoke of the catastrophe, after he recited a *Molei* including the words, "*shenikberu chaim*" ("who were buried alive"), and chanted the *kaddish*, the voice of an eight-year-old girl rose from the rear of the crowd. "Why did they do such a thing?" the innocent child demanded to know.

Until the German invasion in September, 1939, Tarnow was a thriving center of Jewish culture and scholarship, with hundreds of synagogues and houses of learning, and a Jewish population of 25,000 souls. Twenty Jewish men and women were all I could find in Tarnow on my last visit there. Only with great difficulty could a *minyan* be formed for prayer services. Of the five couples considered Jewish in Tarnow, only one contained two spouses whose Jewish origins could be authenticated.

Today, there are no synagogues in Tarnow. The last one was confiscated by Polish authorities, and the Jewish tenants of the community building on Ulica Goldhamera were forced to relocate elsewhere. I visited Abraham Luxemburg, who was confined to bed after a two-week stay in the hospital for kidney surgery. He remembered me from my first visit, and thanked me for the packages of clothing that my wife and I had been sending over the years.

Yosef Sturmwind, Avraham Leistner, Leah Zackicwicz and her daughter, Rzemiana Malgorzata were some of the other Jews that I visited in Tarnow, but most of my time was spent with Abraham Ladner, who guided me around the city and patiently tried to respond to my many questions. Ladner is married to a woman he says is Jewish, an invalid who is cared for by a Red Cross nurse. He showed me his wife's marriage certificate, signed by the *chazzan* of Tarnow. There is no *mezuzah* on the doorpost of Ladner's home because, as he explained to me, he is afraid of the antagonism such a display would arouse. He keeps his *mezuzah* in a drawer, but his *tallit* and *tefilin* are in full view on top of the bureau in his dining room. He prays every day, he assured me, and, indeed, his *talllt* and *tefilin* showed signs of constant use.

Ladner recalled the old days when Krakow (only about seventy kilometers away) had a *shochet*, Abram Lasman, who would come to Tarnow each week to ritually slaughter chickens and occasionally even a cow. Today, there is no *shochet* at all in the entire Poland. Once a month, Ladner goes to Krakow where a *shochet* from Budapest, Hungary arrives to slaughter animals for Jews who wish to observe the dietary laws.

Of the hundreds of *shtiblech*, synagogues, yeshivot, and religious school buildings, the pride of pre-war Tarnow, which had always been filled to capacity, all that remained was the Great Synagogue, capable of accommodating several thousand worshippers. Today, that building, too, is destroyed, and only its *bima* stands exposed in the marketplace.

The *bima*, and the memorial for the 800 Jewish children slaughtered by the Nazis are all that survive of Jewish Tarnow. The Jews of Tarnow are concerned about the fate of this *bima*. For them, it is like the Western Wall, the sole remnant of the ancient Temple. How long would the Polish authorities allow this *bima* to sit exposed in the center of the city? Other Jewish artifacts and buildings have been confiscated, after all. Would it be possible, Ladner wondered, to remove the *bima* to a safe place? And, in an undertone, he asked, ''When it comes to the Jews, *is* there such a thing as a safe place?''

Chapter 23.
A CONVERSATION IN TARNOW

Abraham Ladner, Yossel Berger, and I sat on a bench in the marketplace beside the *bima* of Tarnow, and entered into a heated discussion on whether or not there does, indeed, exist a safe place in this world for the Jewish people. I maintained that the land of Israel is precisely such a haven. During the conversation that ensued, I was deeply impressed with how knowledgeable these two Polish Jews were about Israeli politics, and how passionately they felt about the subject.

Yossel Berger could not understand the leaders of the Jewish state. "What's the use of all the talks and meetings? The Arabs and Jews know very well that there can never be peace between them. If Shamir followed the advice of Sharon, he would strengthen his support within his own party, but what's the point of talking about negotiating with the Palestinians when he knows full well that nothing will ever come of it? Shamir's maneuvering will only cost him the support of his own party."

Ladner interrupted. "Anyone with a head on his shoulders knows that the Arabs will never make peace unless they get their land back. The smarter Arabs will insist on a state of their own. And logic tells us that if the Likud refuses both to return the land and to allow the establishment of an Arab state, there can never be peace. And even if Israel were to return the land and give them their state, the Arabs will still hate the Jews and never be satisfied. There still will not be peace. Thus, things will remain at a standstill. Shamir will continue to argue for a greater Israel without peace, and Peres will argue for a lesser Israel with peace."

At this point, I tried to clarify the issues, pointing out that what my two Polish friends were really advocating was that Shamir state his policy openly and unambiguously. If he wants the Israeli people to support a greater Israel, he must say so distinctly. He must point out that the present situation is dangerous, that trading land for peace would be a grave mistake for Israel, and that the only reasonable exchange that could be made is peace for peace. Those Arabs who object to such an equation must be prepared to face the likely consequences--war. On the other hand, if Shamir does, in fact, want to give the Arabs something in exchange for peace, he must also articulate that policy clearly. But since he cannot offer either the return of land or the establishment of a Palestinian state, and since that is all that might temporarily satisfy some Arabs, then why talk about peace in the first place?

When we returned to our car after our conversation beside the desolate *bima* in the Tarnow marketplace, our driver realized that we were low on gas. We were forced, then, to join a *koleyka*, a gas line, that extended up to two miles. The nearly three-hour wait that followed afforded Yossel Berger with plenty of time to provide me with a good history of Jewish Tarnow.

Tarnow's Jewish history, Yossel Berger reminded me, goes back to the fifteenth century when all the land was in the hands of the *poritzim.* Jews, for their part, were given permission to trade, to own shops, to deal with alcohol, and they were also allowed to have their own synagogue and cemetery.

The Jews and their possessions were secured by the Tarnow municipality. Jews were obliged to pay taxes to the Polish landowners, but the general populace objected to the privileges accorded the Jews, however meager and limited they were. In the eighteenth century, several great fires completely destroyed 23 Jewish buildings. The municipality allowed the Jews to settle then outside of the ghetto, and granted them a four-year tax exemption.

Records show that in 1765, Tarnow had a population of 900 Jews, and seven years later, in 1772, when the city was taken over by Austria, the Jewish population increased to 1,200--about one-third of the population of the entire city. Austria gave the Jews greater freedom, permitting them to develop their skills, so Jews were drawn to Tarnow from other parts of Poland, swelling the city's Jewish population to 1,500, including the Jewish residents of the surrounding villages and towns.

While Jewish life began to flourish in the city, Tarnow was also the place where a blood libel occurred in which a Jew was accused of killing a Christian child to use his blood for the Passover *matzot*. When the real murderer was found, the Jew was released. In 1842, a Jewish hospital was constructed in Tarnow, and in 1890, with the financial backing of Baron de Hirsch, a Jewish school was opened that continued in operation until the outbreak of the First World War in 1914.

Tarnow was an important center of *chassidic* life in Poland, the home of the Tarnobrzeg Dzhikever Rebbe. There were also many *maskilim*, including the well-known Hebrew writer, Mordechai David Brandster. In addition, religious and secular Zionism were very popular in Tarnow. Records show the existence in 1891 of an organization called *Ahavat Zion*, whose aim was settlement in Palestine as a Galician community.

The Jews of Tarnow were primarily manufacturers of hats and garments. After World War I, when Tarnow reverted to Polish rule, the economic situation deteriorated and many Jews were forced to subsist on public welfare. But the Jewish population of Tarnow was always sizable in relation to the general Polish population of the city. In 1880, there were over 11,000 Jews in Tarnow, 46 percent of the total population. By 1939, there were 25,000 Jews in Tarnow; 55 percent of the city's population was Jewish. One of the leaders of the community was Abraham Chomet, whose *Sefer Zikaron* was published in Israel after the war.

On September 8, 1939, the Nazi armies captured the city of Tarnow. Immediately, they began to terrorize the Jewish community. As soon as Auschwitz was opened in 1940, the three leaders of Tarnow Jewry, Emil Wieder, Isaac Holzer, and Maximilian Rosenbush, were among the first victims of the camp.

The Tarnow ghetto went into operation in March 1941. In June 1942, Jews from the surrounding area were forced into the Tarnow ghetto. The Nazis deported 12,000 Jews for extermination in Belzec. The ghetto was then divided into two parts, Ghetto A, a forced labor camp, and Ghetto B, for families. Many in the Tarnow ghetto perished of hunger.

In September 1942, an additional 8,000 Jews were deported to Belzec to be exterminated. Two months later, on November 15, 3,000 more were killed. On September 2, 1943, 5,000 Jews were sent to Auschwitz and 3,000 to Plaszow concentration camps. About 500 Jews who were found hiding were shot, and the last 300 were sent to Plaszow, where most of them died.

After the war, 700 Jews attempted to return to their homes in Tarnow. They were attacked by the Polish citizenry, as were many other Polish Jews who attempted to reclaim their lost homes and property after the war. The Jews left the city of Tarnow, and today, only a poor handful remains.

Chapter 24.
RZESZOW

The long lines in Poland to buy food, gasoline, and other necessities make shopping a major activity in this poor country. Often, people stand in line for hours, only to find empty shelves when their turn comes to enter the store, or to be told, "Sorry, no more benzine" when they finally reach the gas pump. We were lucky enough to get sufficient gas to return to Krakow. At my suggestion, our driver filled the tank that night, when the lines are shorter, so that early the next morning we were ready to set out for the city of Rzeszow.

Rzeszow (or Reischa, as it is called in Yiddish, and Risha in Hebrew) is a city located between Tarnow and Przemysl. Like many other Galician towns and cities, the land had been the exclusive property of the local *poretz*, in this case, the Lubomisky family, which controlled the area until 1792, when Austria annexed this section of Poland. The first records attesting to the construction of a Jewish synagogue and cemetery in Rzeszow date to the seventeenth century.

One thousand Jews lived in Rzeszow at the beginning of the eighteenth century when a controversy erupted between the Jews of Rzeszow and Przemysl concerning Rabbi Yechezkel Yehoshua Feivel Frenkel-Teumin, who was first rabbi of Przemysl and then moved to Rzeszow. The Przemysl community then removed him from his position as rabbi of the province and replaced him with Rabbi Samuel Mendelowicz of Lvov. This controversy was debated at the convention of the provincial council of Przemysl in 1715, as well as at a meeting at Jaroslaw, which was within the framework of the *Vaad Arba Arazot* (the Council of the Four Lands) to which Rzeszow belonged. The Rzeszow community broke away from the provincial council and also declared itself an independent entity in relation to the *Vaad Arba Arazot.*

The Jews of Rzeszow were the principal manufacturers and owners of the goldsmith and textile industry. They were also skilled seal engravers. The city of Rzeszow was referred to as "Little Jerusalem" because of its religious population. It boasted *chassidim* as well as *maskilim.* Rabbi Yaakov Reischer (his name is derived from the Yiddish pronunciation of Rzeszow) headed a yeshiva and was the author of many volumes on *halacha*, including *Minchat Yaakov* on the Rema's *Torat Hachatatt*, as well as *Chok L'Yaakov* on the laws of Passover, and *Shevut Yaakov.* Of interest in this latter volume is a section entitled, *"Lo hibit aven b'Yaakov,"* which is a reply to those who attacked him for his earlier works.

Rabbis who have difficulties with their congregations would perhaps empathize with Rabbi Reischer's account of his problems. In 1715, when Rabbi Reischer became chief justice of the rabbinic court of Worms and students flocked to study at his yeshiva, members of his community persecuted him. In 1718, in Metz, where he also served as chief justice and the head of the yeshiva, he again found no peace. Rabbi Reischer writes: "Malicious men hard as iron hated me without cause and set upon me to destroy me with false libel so that I would be imprisoned." The last chief rabbi of Rzeszow before the outbreak of the war was Rabbi Lewin, the popular leader of the Agudat Israel movement and a member of the Polish *Sejm.*

Before the war, 14,000 Jews lived in Rzeszow. Today there is not a single Jew left in the city. When the Germans occupied the city in 1939, they immediately set to work instituting their evil design. The ghetto was established in 1941, and during the five days between July seventh and July thirteenth, 14,000 Jews were deported from the neighboring towns and villages. About 8,000 Rzeszow Jews were exterminated in Belzec. Several hundred who resisted were shot. One thousand Jews were executed in the nearby Rudna forest, and, a month later, another thousand women and children were taken from the ghetto to the Peikinia concentration camp and murdered. Three thousand Jews who remained in the ghetto became part of a forced labor camp divided into two sections: Section A for slave laborers, and Section B, for their families.

The Rzeszow ghetto was liquidated between September and November 1943. The first group of deportees was sent to the Szebnia forced labor camp where they perished. The second group was murdered at Auschwitz.

During the German occupation of Rzeszow, the Catholic bishop of the city confiscated many Jewish artifacts and religious articles, promising to open a museum in which these items would be displayed. When I visited the city, I arranged to meet with this gentleman to inquire about the whereabouts of these articles, most of which belonged to the Bobover chassidim. The bishop informed me that an emissary from the Vatican had come and taken everything away. From its expropriation of goods and artifacts, to its conversion of thousands of Jewish children during the War, to its unforgivable silence as the Nazis carried out their atrocities, the Catholic church has a great deal of self-examination and penance to do.

Chapter 25.
ROPCZYCE AND LANCUT

Ropczyce, or Ropschitz as it is known in Yiddish, is another of those Polish towns that once boasted a lively Jewish community and is now utterly bereft of its Jews. Jews lived in this small town between Tarnow and Rzeszow from the sixteenth century, though for a period of time, they were banned from residing in Ropczyce as a result of a decree by King Sigismund who was responding to the local merchants' fear of Jewish competition. The decree was nullified by King John Kazimierz the Second, and Jewish life continued unabated in Ropczyce until the war. At one time, there were 1,000 Jewish residents in the town, but by the time the Ropschitzer Tzaddik died in 1827 the number had already decreased, and by 1921 the Jewish population of Ropczyce had dwindled to three hundred.

The Ropchitzer Tzaddik, Rabbi Naftali Ropchitzer, was a well-known chassidic leader, the student of Rabbi Mendel Rimanover, Rabbi Elimelech of Lyzhensk, and the Chozeh of Lublin, and the teacher of Rabbi Chaim Halberstam, known as the Sanzer Tzaddik. At one point, there was a difference of opinion between the Ropchitzer Tzaddik and his teacher, Rabbi Mendel Rimanover on the subject of the benefits to the Jews of the Napoleonic victories. The Rimanover maintained that Napoleon's triumphs marked the beginning of the emancipation and, ultimately, of the redemption. The Ropchitzer, for his part, expressed a deep fear of the assimilation that would ensue as a result of Jewish service in the military and Jewish youth attending gentile schools.

The Ropschitzer Tzaddik was known for his kindly sense of humor. For example, he was reported to have once approached a Jew who had just completed praying the *Shmoneh Esreh* and to have greeted him with a hearty *shalom aleichem*. When the Jew objected that such a greeting was usually reserved for an individual whom one had not seen for a while or for a person who had just returned from a long trip, the Ropschitzer Tzaddik replied,'' Tell me, what were you thinking of when you were saying the *Shmoneh Esreh?* No doubt you attended some markets in Krakow or Lublin and you returned at the end of the prayer. In that case, you've certainly earned a *shalom aleichem*.''

On another occasion, Rabbi Naftali Ropschitzer returned home after making his *Shabbat HaGadol* sermon and appeal. "How did you do?'' his wife inquired. "Fifty-fifty,'' replied the Ropschitzer Tzaddik. "The poor are ready to take, but whether the rich are prepared to give, I'm not so sure.''

The Germans entered Ropczyce on September 7, 1939. Immediately, they set fire to the main synagogue and its Torah scrolls. All the Jewish residents of the town were sent to forced labor and their property was confiscated. A ghetto existed in Ropczyce for a short period of time, but was liquidated on July 2, 1942 when most of the Jewish population was deported to the Belzec extermination camp and the rest were shot in the town. Not a single Jew can be found in Ropczyce today, and even the cemetery is impossible to locate.

Lancut is another town in the greater Krakow area, located seventeen miles from Rzeszow, on Route E40. According to my guide, Yossel Berger, an organized Jewish community already existed in Lancut in the seventeenth century with its own synagogue and cemetery. It is recorded that several dozen Sephardic Jewish immigrants from various Middle Eastern countries had settled in Lancut. In the eighteenth century, the Jews of Lancut suffered from the edict issued by the Bishop of Przemysl prohibiting Jews from celebrating weddings on Sundays and Christian holidays, and forcing Jews to close their shops whenever the Catholic priest rode by in his carriage ringing his bell as a signal to the devout to kneel before the passing procession.

Among the great Jewish scholars and rabbis of Lancut were Rabbi Yaakov Yitzchak Horowitz, later known as the Chozeh of Lublin, Rabbi Moshe Tzvi Hirsch Meislich, and Rabbi Aryeh Leibush. For forty years during the nineteenth century, the Dinever Rabbi Tzvi Elimelech, the *Benei Yissachar*, son of Rabbi Eliezer Shapiro, occupied the rabbinic position in Lancut, and it was in this period, in 1860, that a Jewish cemetery was dedicated in the town. Despite the anti-Semitism of the local citizenry, the Jews of Lancut, constituting about 50 percent of the total population of 3,000, thrived until the war, with synagogues and houses of learning serving the needs of the community, and a wide variety of chassidim, followers of the rabbis of Dzikov, Bobov, Belz, Radomsk, and others.

On September 9, 1939, the Germans marched into Lancut, set the synagogue on fire, and ordered the Jews into forced labor. By the twenty-second of September, most of Lancut's Jewish population had been driven across the San River to Russia, while the rest were scattered among other Polish towns under German occupation. About 1,000 Jews returned to Lancut in the early part of 1940, and in the middle of the following year, after Russia joined the Allies against Germany, many of the Jews who had been forced into Russia returned to their hometown to rejoin their families. Of these returning Jews, many were caught and shot. In August, 1942, the Jews of Lancut were herded into the forest and shot. Only fifty Jews remained, and they were taken to the Shiniwa ghetto. When the Shiniwa ghetto was liquidated, all of these Jews were taken to the cemetery and murdered. There is not a single Jew left in Lancut today. The synagogue is now a museum, and the cemetery is in poor condition.

About ten miles outside of the city of Jaroslaw we passed the small town of Przeworsk. I had heard of this town from my father, who spoke often of its righteous and learned men. In 1498, Przeworsk was overrun by the Turks; Jews were already settling there at that early date. At one time Rabbi Moshe Sofer served as the spiritual leader of the town. In *Noam Elimelech*, by the great *tzaddik*, Rabbi Elimelech of Lizhensk, there is an account of *haskamot* (approvals) by two rabbis connected with the town of Przeworsk. The first is dated 5548 (approximately 200 years ago) and is signed by Rabbi Shmuel HaKatan, the son of Rabbi Moshe Pinchas, the chief justice of the rabbinic court of Przeworsk. The second approval, written in the same year, was signed by the *mekubal*, Rabbi Avraham Moshe, son of Tzvi Hirsch of Przeworsk. In 1930, there was a great fire in Przeworsk, which destroyed many Jewish homes and businesses, rendering much of the populace homeless and forcing them to turn to charitable institutions for assistance. At that time there were 2,000 Jews in Przeworsk. Today there is none. I was unable to even find the cemetery. The local citizenry, noting my yarmulke, greeted me coldly and with contempt. Even one Jew was too many for them. I left Przeworsk as soon as I could, and continued on my way.

Chapter 26.
JAROSLAW

Jaroslaw near the San River was included in the six districts formed by the Nazi, Krueger, on October 28, 1942. These six districts took in the areas of Krakow, Bochnia, Tarnow, Rzeszow, Debica, and Prezmysl, and were officially part of the greater Krakow district. Soon after the formation of the six districts, 100,000 Jews from the area were murdered in cold blood. Krueger organized twenty forced labor camps, among them Plaszow in the Krakow district, which was eventually converted into a killing center.

Beyond Jaroslaw, the Galicia district was formed, taking in a number of cities, including Tarnopol, Lemberg, Stanislaw, and others. During the High Holidays of 1941, the Nazis marched 10,000 Jews from this district, including many Jews from Przemysl of the Krakow district, into one of the cemeteries and shot them all. By the end of 1942, 350,000 Jews in the area had been murdered.

All this was merely a continuation of German policy put into place immediately after the invasion of Poland on September 1, 1939. Eight days after the invasion, the Nazi, Hans Frank, ordered all Jewish shopkeepers to display the Star of David in their store windows. In short order, 20,000 Jews were killed, 50,000 Jewish homes, factories, and businesses in over 120 counties were destroyed, and 30 percent of Jewish homes were bombed or set on fire. Jews from small towns and villages sought refuge in the larger cities. Within a brief period of time, 32,000 Jewish soldiers were killed while 60,000 were taken prisoner and eventually died in Nazi prison camps.

The degradation of Jews was also part of the Nazi program. This included public cutting off of beards with blunt instruments, often tearing the flesh; setting beards on fire; forcing one Jew to crawl on his hands and knees while another rode on his back; compelling Jews to wrestle with each other for the amusement and sport of the German soldiers. The Sabbath or Jewish holidays were usually deliberately chosen for the staging of these sadistic entertainments.

The Nazis also set buildings on fire, prohibiting anyone from attempting to extinguish the flames, and shooting on the spot any individual who sought to flee from the conflagration. To publicly absolve themselves of the crime, the Nazis then forced the rabbis to sign a document confessing to the arson. Any Jew who dared to enter a burning synagogue to rescue a Torah scroll was shot or allowed to burn to death. In the center of the marketplace, the Nazis burned holy books and sacred articles of all sorts, forcing Jews to sing merry songs and dance around the fire.

Of the three and one half million Jews who lived in Poland when the war began, two million fell immediately under Hitler's domination while the remaining million and one half were under the control of the Russian forces. When hostilities broke out between Germany and Russia in 1941, all three and one half million Polish Jews came under German control. Poland was then divided into five districts--Warsaw, Lublin, Radom, Krakow, and Galicia--which, in turn, were further divided into smaller districts.

Jaroslaw and Przemysl were included in the Krakow district. Jaroslaw is part of the Rzeszow province, about twenty miles from Przemysl along Route 40. In the sixteenth and seventeenth centuries, Jaroslaw was known for its great fairs held three times a year. The major fair took place in September, around the time of the High Holidays. Jews participated in this fair, particularly in the sale of oxen and other domestic animals. Providing their own security for Jewish merchants, Jews played an important role in Polish enterprise through their participation in these fairs.

There were special Jewish courts in Jaroslaw with judges known as *Dayanei Hayerid*. Each Jewish merchant was obligated to pay a tax to these courts to keep them in operation. Meetings of the *Vaad Arba Arazot* were often held in Jaroslaw during the fair at which *cherems* (excommunications) were occasionally issued. A temporary synagogue was established to provide needed services for Jewish merchants, and to draw Jewish visitors to the city. This amenity is documented in one of the responsa (Number 84) of a Rabbi Meir of Lublin: "It happened that we were in the city of Jaroslaw at the fair of 1608 where it was a regular custom, as it is at every fair, that a place be set aside as a synagogue to pray every day and also on the Sabbath so that the scholars and heads of the yeshivot and leaders of the land, as well as others, gathered to read the Torah, as is customary in the communities. And since the town is near the community of Przemysl, they conveyed from there the Torah scroll belonging to that town's congregation."

Jews began to settle in Jaroslaw in the middle of the seventeenth century and immediately built a synagogue in the town, although a cemetery was not established until 1699. In 1787, a blood libel in Jaroslaw resulted in the murder of many Jews as well as in the suicide, following extreme torture, of the Jew who had been falsely accused of killing a gentile child and using the blood to bake *matzot*. Records disclose that one hundred Jewish families resided in Jaroslaw in 1738; a century later, there were 2,300 Jews living in the city.

By the 1930's, 7,000 Jews lived in Jaroslaw. The city had become a center of Jewish learning and culture, both secular and religious. The Nazi armies invaded Jaroslaw on September 10, 1939. Following their customary procedure, the Nazis levied a huge fine on the Jewish community, and, to insure payment, arrested the leaders, including the *rosh hakahal*, Mendel Reich. At the end of September, the Jews of Jaroslaw as well as thousands from the surrounding towns and villages were ordered to the the city's sports field. From there, they were driven across the San river to the Russian side. Robbed of all their belongings, they penetrated deeper and deeper into Russia, without realizing at the time that in this way their lives would be saved. Those who remained at the border were murdered when war broke out between Germany and Russia. Those who stayed in Jaroslaw were deported to Belzec where they were annihilated.

At the police station in Jaroslaw, I received the same reply to my old question: "Where are the Jews?" "*Niema Zhydy.*" "No Jews," the officer in charge informed me. By now, my question had become a mournful refrain; the reply, a heartbreaking elegy.

Chapter 27.
PRZEMYSL

I have a special soft spot in my heart for Przemysl because my brother, Yechezkel Shragai (named for the Shiniver Rebbe, Rabbi Yechezkel Shragai Halberstam), and his wife, Mania, lived there for more than ten years. He was very active in Jewish community affairs, and both his house and his store were on Ulica Peretza 3, not far from the San River which marked the German-Russian border until 1941. Our family in the United States heard from Yechezkel Shragai until the beginning of 1943. After the war we tried to find out what had become of him. My oldest sister, Chaya Yehudit, together with her husband, Moshe Meyer Ziegeltuch and their family, had left Krakow to stay with our brother in Przemysl. They were hoping for the best. All of them perished.

At the Przemysl police station, there was no record of my brother's street or address. Mrs. Roza Fellner, now seventy-six years old but still very active, remembered the neighborhood and very kindly accompanied me there. As we walked around the town together, I could barely keep up with her. "What's your hurry?" I asked. "I haven't much time, you know," she explained. "I'm seventy-six, going on seventy-seven."

Our taxi took us to what had been Ulica Peretza. "This was the street," Mrs. Fellner said. Nothing remained; there were no buildings, no roads, only abandoned stretches of land as far as the eye could see. It had become a no-man's land in 1939 when the German-Russian border was demarcated, and all the existing structures had been destroyed. The area was never rebuilt.

Przemysl is located in the Rzeszow province of eastern Galicia, near the present Polish-Russian border. From 1772 to 1919, the city was under Austrian rule, as was the entire Galicia. Records show that Przemysl already existed as a city in the fourteenth century and that eighteen Jewish families lived there as early as 1542. By 1775, the Jewish population of Przemysl had increased to 1,600 people.

In 1625, the rabbi of Przemysl was known to be Simon Wolf. In *Zhydi w Przemysl* (1903), M. Schorr writes that in 1578, during the rule of the Polish King Stefan Batory, Jewish crafts developed rapidly in Przemysl. A Jew called Calman was popular as an expert tanner and furrier, and was granted special permission from the king to ply his trade. Despite these concessions, however, and despite the small number of Jews living in the city, anti-Semitism was prevalent. According to reports from that period, "Jews totally ruined the goldsmiths', tailors', butchers' and bakers' guilds, and they eradicated the barbers' 'blood-letters' guild. Several Jewish barbers accompanied doctors on visits to patients for the purpose of blood-letting which was done by applying cups to an incised vein to remove some of the blood."

There was a Jewish tailors' guild in Przemysl, a "*chevra kadisha d'malbushei arumim,*" a holy society for those who dress the naked. The laws governing *shatness* were strictly enforced by this guild under the supervision of the community and its rabbis.

The Jewish population of Przemysl in the 1930's, prior to the war, was 20,000 souls. Many Jews were involved in the wheat and timber industries as well as in banking and agriculture. In 1928, eighteen of the forty seats in the municipal administration council were won by Jews, and a Jew was elected deputy mayor of the city. That year, the Agudat Israel party received the majority vote, while in 1936 the majority was won by the General Zionists, whose leader, Jacob Rebhan, was elected president of the community organization, a position he retained until the outbreak of the war three years later. Another well-known community leader and activist of this pre-war period was Moshe Sheinbach.

Among the popular and well-regarded rabbis of Przemysl were Rabbi Shmuel Heller and Rabbi Yitzchak Schmelkes, a Talmudic scholar from Lemberg who was a disciple of Rabbi Shaul Yossef Natanson. His six-volume *Bet Yitzchak* on the four sections of the *Shulchan Aruch* is known to all students of *halacha*. Although he was a member of the Mizrachi party, his ideas influenced Jewish thought across the spectrum. Until 1939, there were also several chassidic rabbis in Przemysl.

The Germans entered Przemysl on September 14, 1939. Within several days, 500 Jews were murdered after having been accused of killing twelve Germans. Russia soon took over a section of the city, while the Jews of Zasanie (those on the other side of the San River) remained under German rule. In 1940, 7,000 Jews were transferred to the Russian side of the city. When Germany occupied the entire city in 1941, a *Judenrat* was set up headed by Ignacy Duldig. About one year later, on August 3, 1943, 12,000 Jews were deported to the Belzec extermination camp. In September, 3,000 Jews were sent to Auschwitz. Another deportation of 4,000 Jews to Belzec took place on the eighth of November. Soon afterward, the 2,000 remaining Jews of Przemysl were murdered.

An attempt at a revolt against the German occupiers was quickly suppressed and all the participants were shot. Przemysl was recaptured by the Russians on July 27, 1944. After the war, 2,000 Jewish refugees returned to the city and tried to organize a community council under the leadership of Tzvi Rubenfeld and Mordechai Shattner. This organized effort lasted only a short while and was soon disbanded.

During my first visit to Przemysl, there were fifty Jews residing in the city with a synagogue and a *minyan* on the Sabbath and holidays. Thirty years later, only five Jews could be identified in Przemysl:
Shimon Boksman, Ulica Maya 54
Roza Fellner, Ulica Smolni 6
Barbara Feuchtenbaum, Ulica Dworckiego 2
Yoachim Glattner, Ulica Wybrzeze Kosciusky 36/14
Erna Gletner, Ulica Tuvima 5/3
The Jewish cemetery in Przemysl is still in use and is in fair condition. There are no longer any synagogues in Przemysl, though several *pomniks* (monuments) can be found in the city, commemorating the Jewish life that had once been there and is no more.

Left: Chazan Michael Gutter
reciting prayer at Sanz Cemetary

Below: Entering the city of
Przemysl

Left: Admor Rav Benzion Halberstam,
the Bobover Rebbe

Above: The Warsaw "Free Kitchen"

Right: Beth Mederash of Bobover Rebbe in Bove, now a trade school

Above: Former residence of Bobover Rebbe

Above: Admor Rav Shlolomo Halberstam, the Bobover Rebbe Brooklyn

Above: Monument to remember the Sosnowiec and Bedzin ghetto Jews who were murdered

Chapter 28.
A MEETING IN WARSAW WITH LEADERS OF
THE JEWISH COMMUNITY

Having been notified by Chief Rabbi Pinchas Menachem Joskowicz that a special meeting of community leaders from all over Poland would be convened in Warsaw the next day, I bid farewell to my new friends in Przemysl and boarded the eight o'clock train that evening, hoping to arrive at my destination no later than midnight. However, the Polish transportation system being what it is, I arrived in Warsaw at 6:30 the next morning after a restless night on the *Nachtzug*, a journey that cost 3,500 zlotys, or about 60 or 70 cents.

At the time of my trip to Poland, the official exchange rate was 700 or 800 zlotys to the dollar, though even public banks were offering the black market rate of 4,000 zlotys. By trading in the streets near the Forum or Intercontinental Hotel, however, an American could get between 6,000 and 7,000 zlotys for his dollar. These transactions, however, were fraught with peril, as my guide informed me, because after the Polish trader offers an excellent rate of exchange and actually counts out the zlotys in front of you, he takes advantage of the moment that you are reaching into your wallet and extracting the agreed-upon amount of dollars. During that interval, he quickly switches the packet of zlotys he has shown you for one containing far fewer bills. By the time you realize that you have received 20 percent of the promised money, the con man has long since disappeared into the crowd.

When I arrived at the Warsaw synagogue at about 7:15 that morning, I found Rabbi Joskowicz there along with most of the *asara batlanim*, the ten men available for a quorum, to whom the rabbi pays a small stipend in order to make sure that there will be a *minyan* for services. As the day progressed, I had an opportunity to meet privately with each of the community leaders and to learn many interesting facts about what remains of Jewish life in Poland.

The head of the **Warsaw** Jewish community is Dr. Simcha Weiss. He informed me that in Warsaw today there are between 700 and 800 Jews, of whom only about 100 are affiliated with the synagogue. Dr. Weiss estimates that the entire Jewish population of present-day Poland is approximately 7,000.

The Warsaw synagogue houses not only the *shul* itself and its administrative offices, but also accommodations for visitors, as well as the main offices of the Polish Jewish community, the chief rabbi's office, the offices of the president, vice-president, and general secretary, and a vestry room in which all meetings take place. Services are held on the Sabbath, holidays, and the first day of each new month. Few women attend.

Kosher meals are served to sixty or seventy persons, among them an occasional non-Jew. No questions are asked. The meals are free, donated by the Joint Distribution Committee. There is a *bikkur cholim* society to visit the sick, and to help and support them in any way possible. A concert of cantorial music is held each month, attended by an audience of several hundred people, Jews and non-Jews. With the arrival of the new chief rabbi, a daily *minyan* has been instituted.

At the time of my visit, a *chevra kadisha* was being organized to attend to the preparation of the dead for burial. The rabbi teaches a class in *Mishna*, and delivers a sermon every Sabbath after the *Musaf* prayers. Following the Sabbath services, the congregants are invited to attend a *kiddush* in which the traditional array of food and drink is offered. The synagogue is in need of more prayer books, prayer shawls, and Bibles. The Warsaw Jewish cemetery, Dr. Weiss informed me, is maintained in good order.

The leader of the **Krakow** Jewish community is Czeslaw Jakbowicz. There are two synagogues in Krakow: the Remu Synagogue on Ulica Szeroka, which seats approximately 75 people, and the Temple, formerly known as Dr. Thon's Shul, on Ulica Miodowa 24. The latter is a huge edifice, capable of accommodating many hundreds of worshippers. Today it is used only on the High Holidays or when large groups of tourists arrive to visit. It is now in the process of being remodeled. In the Temple yard there is a *mikvah* which is kept heated for those who wish to immerse themselves in its waters.

There are 560 Jews officially registered in Krakow, but only 10 percent belong to the congregation, and only about 10 or 15 percent attend services on the Sabbath and holidays. No one is skilled in reading from the Torah, so the weekly portion is read from the *Chumash* unless a visitor is available who is capable of chanting from the scroll. A *kiddush* is offered every Sabbath and on holidays after services. Forty to fifty Joint Distribution lunches are served daily. The Jewish cemetery of Krakow is well maintained.

Shmuel Shuster is the head of the **Szczecin** Jewish community. There is no synagogue left in Szczecin but services are held in a private home. Mr. Shuster is the only person who leads the prayers. Although there are several hundred Jews in the city, only 76 belong to the congregation. Services are conducted on the Sabbath, holidays, and the first day of the new month, with about fifteen worshippers attending. The Jewish community has four children under the age of thirteen, but only three men are married to Jewish women. There is only one functional cemetery in Szczecin, and both Jews and non-Jews are buried here in separate sections.

The leader of the **Katowice** Jewish community, Felix Lippman, lives in nearby Sosnowiec, which, at present, has only seven Jews though it does have its own Jewish cemetery. The total Jewish population of Katowice is 600, with 120 who are officially affiliated with the congregation. The city boasts a large *bet-medrash* in which Sabbath and holiday services are held, attended by about twenty to thirty worshippers. What is unusual about the Jewish community of Katowice is that there are 25 young Jews between the ages of four and thirty. However, there is no *Talmud Torah* to provide for their Jewish education. Very few Jews are married to fellow Jews. The Katowice cemetery is in good order.

Shmuel Farber, the head of the Jewish community in **Gliwice**, who lives in the nearby town of Zabrze, informed me that Gliwice has a nice synagogue in which services are held on the Sabbath, holidays, and the first day of the new month. Of a total population of 100 Jews, only ten attend services. There are four children in Gliwice under the age of fifteen, a fenced-in cemetery, and intermarriage is prevalent in the community.

From Moses Finkelstein, the leader of the entire Polish Jewish community, I gathered the following information about remaining synagogues and places of worship:

In **Bielsko-Byala**, there is no synagogue, but services are held at Ulica Mickewicza 26 whenever a *minyan* can be gathered.

In **Bytom**, there is a synagogue on Ulica Plac Grunwaldzki 62.

In **Dzierzoniow**, there is a synagogue on Ulica Krasickiego 28.

In **Legnica**, there is a synagogue on Ulica Choynowska 17.

In **Lodz**, there is a synagogue on Ulica Zachodnia 78.

In **Walbrzych**, prayer services are conducted in a private home on Ulica Mickiewicza 18.

In **Przyrow**, services are held in a private home on Ulica Lelowska 2.

In **Wroclaw**, they pray at Ulica Wlodkowicza 9.

In all of Poland there are six or seven functioning synagogues, and nine or ten private homes in which services are occasionally conducted. This is all that remains in a country that once was a thriving center of Jewish religious and spiritual life.

Chapter 29.
ON THE ROAD TO BOBOWA

My guide, Yossel Berger, responded with great enthusiasm when I informed him that I intended to visit Bobowa, which had once been a flourishing center of chassidic life. I mentioned to him that I had already been to the cemetery where the Chozeh of Lublin is interred, and he commented fervently, "Ah, a great *tzaddik*--a prophet, a seer!" He had read a great deal about the Chozeh of Lublin and had escorted many visitors to the grave of this illustrious sage. He had stood by as men and women wept and prayed at the graveside, and had observed how relieved and hopeful they had seemed when they completed their supplications.

The Chozeh of Lublin, Yossel Berger reminded me, was able to reveal the genealogy of a person's soul and to discern the restitution of the soul in each of its stages of reincarnation. It was in recognition of this gift, as well as for his ability to predict future events, that, after his death, Rabbi Yaakov Yitzchak Horowitz was called the *Chozeh*--the prophet-- of Lublin. He was a student of some of the great chassidic masters-- Rabbi Dov Ber of Mezericz, Rabbi Levi Yitzchak of Berdichev, and Rabbi Elimelech of Lyzensk.

Of particular interest to my guide, Yossel Berger, was the Chozeh's insistence that before an individual could properly do *teshuva*, before he could truly repent, it was necessary for him to earn a comfortable livelihood. Only after a person's physical needs were adequately provided for could he truly worship God. According to the Chozeh, when a body enjoys plenty, the soul, in turn, can partake of spiritual riches. For the Chozeh, scholarship was important, but love of fellow man was perhaps of greater significance. The Chozeh was convinced that the Napoleonic campaigns and the wars with England represented the Battle of Gog and Magog and the beginning of the redemption of the Jewish people.

In this fashion, relating to each other the histories and legends of chassidic masters, Yossel Berger and I traveled along Highway 40 toward Tarnow, and from there turned south to Bobowa. As we drew nearer to our destination, I was increasingly overcome with a sense that I was returning to my roots, for as a child, I had been brought up as a Bobover chassid. The Bobover rebbe at the time, Reb Benzion Halberstam, had made his court in Trzebinia, not far from my hometown of Oswiecim. On the holiday of Succot, my brother Lippe and I would travel to Trzebinia, to bask in the the Rebbe's holy presence. Lippe is, to this day, an ardent Bobover chassid in Borough Park, a loyal follower of the present Bobover Rebbe, Reb Shlomo Halberstam, the son of Rabbi Benzion Halberstam of Trzebinia.

How vividly I remember the spiritual impressions and sense of awe that overwhelmed me on *Isru Chag Succot*, as I stood, a young boy, before the Bobover Rebbe in his chambers. I recall how he spoke to me with such deep love and affection, it was as if I were his own child. Trembling I stood before him, awaiting my "sentence" as to which Etz Chaim Bobover yeshiva I would be sent to. And, with profound dread, I waited to see which apple he would choose for me from the heap of apples that had been taken down from the *succah* the night before and been collected in a large box beside his seat.

The Rebbe gave each visitor one of three types of apples. The first was beautiful both outside and inside, like a perfect *etrog*. The second had an ugly surface, but within it was delicious and sweet. The third apple was beautiful externally, but inside it was rotten. It was believed that the Rebbe possessed *Ruach Hakodesh*, divine inspiration, and the type of apple he chose for each individual would reveal that person's true nature. I remember how, as a child, I refused to show my apple to anyone, even to my brother Lippe, who was so close to me. It was truly uncanny how the Rebbe was able to fit my apple to my character and my behavior, to my very soul.

Before my first return trip to Poland thirty years ago, I came to the present-day Bobover Rebbe, Rabbi Shlomo Halberstam, to request a blessing for success on my mission. One of my major concerns at the time was to locate some of the hundreds of Jewish boys and girls who remained scattered all over Poland after the war in gentile homes, monasteries, and convents. Our aim was to rescue as many of them as possible and return them to Jewish life in America or Israel.

The Rebbe's blessing did, indeed, help me, for we were successful in identifying and saving some of these lost souls. But what I recall most vividly from that visit was how the Rebbe's eyes lit up when I mentioned that I would be stopping at his hometown of Bobowa. "Bobov! My *shtetl* Bobov! Once it was a holy town!" He then proceeded to give me precise directions, signs, and even secrets about the *bet-medrash*, the *mikvah*, and the courtyard of the former Rebbe.

When I returned to the United States after that visit, I gave an account to the Rebbe of all I had seen and heard. The old Bobover *bet-medrash* had been taken over by the municipality and had been converted into a trade school under the direction of a Mr. Czisek. The information with which the Rebbe had entrusted me had been so accurate it had been almost impossible to make a mistake. I had no difficulty at all in finding what I was looking for because the signs and signals were so clear.

Chapter 30.
THE BOBOV BET-MEDRASH

"Here is a villa where a wealthy Jew once lived," my taxi driver said as we entered the outskirts of Bobowa. "On the other side of the road was a large mill that had once belonged to a Jew," he continued. "That area was a place where Jewish merchants sold their wares to Polish peasants," he went on. Staring out the window as we drove past each of these sights, I couldn't help wondering if my driver was going on with this mournful litany out of a desire to be helpful and informative, or out of a compulsion to demonstrate how completely Jewish life had been purged from the town.

The roofs of the small Bobover *chatkes* (homes) began to appear on the horizon. Minutes later, the driver announced, "This is the town of Bobowa." He parked the taxi in the marketplace and we proceeded on foot. As I stepped out of the car, a rock thrown by some unknown hand struck the windshield. Welcome, Jew, to Bobowa!

An old gentile wearing a fur hat approached and greeted us with a friendly "*Dzien dobry*" (good day). "Are you looking for the *Rabin's* house?" he asked. Grabbing hold of my hand, he surprised me with a "*Shalom aleichem,*" spoken in a Polish accent. He remembered the old Bobover Rebbe as well as his son, he told me, and he remembered, too, the Rebbe's home where hundreds, and sometimes thousands of chassidim from all over western Galicia would gather for the Jewish holidays. From the Yiddish words interspersed in the old man's conversation, I gathered that he must have had close contact with the

Jews of the town. Perhaps he had been a *"Shabbos Goy"* in the old days, whose job it was to come into the house on the Sabbath and remove the candlesticks, keep the furnace stoked, turn off the lights, or bring in the *cholent* from the bakery. For the performance of these chores, he would receive some white *challah* from the mistress of the house and a gracious *dzienkuje*, thank you.

"Come," said the old man, "I will take you to the *Rabin's* house." We followed him in and out of a series of narrow streets. The houses seemed unchanged; only those who dwelled within them were different. There are no Jews left in Bobowa today. When the Germans took over Poland, Jewish life in Bobowa was decimated.

"*Gdzie jest syn Rabina*?" the old man inquired. "Where is the Rabbi's son?" I turned around and noticed that we had attracted a crowd of about half a dozen men who were following us as we made our way through the town. This group would comprise an excellent audience for what I had to say.

"The Rabbi's son," I announced, "is today one of the best-known leaders of thousands of Bobover chassidim in the United States and in Israel. His synagogue in Brooklyn is many times larger than the one in Bobowa. In Israel there is a city called Bobov where thousands of his followers live, and where there are schools providing every level of religious instruction."

The little crowd stared at me in open-mouthed amazement. The old man's lips began to move within the parentheses of his drooping mustache. "It is almost fifty years since Bobowa has had no Jews," he said sadly. "Everything is dead in this town. We used to buy from them and sell to them. They were our best customers. We miss the Jews. We used to go to the *Rabin* to ask his blessings, for the Bobover Rebbe was truly a holy man."

One of the younger men interrupted the old man's flow of reminiscences and fond recollections of the Jews. "Here is the *Rabin's* house!" the younger man declared. Indeed, it was the very same two-story building that I remembered from before the war. The large *bet-medrash*, which had once been the center for Bobover chassidim in western Galicia, was now a Polish trade school. On my first return visit, I remember seeing Polish youths working at carpentry and other manual trades. At the Eastern wall, where the Rebbe's chair, on which no one dared to sit, was placed, and where the walls had been lined with cases containing holy books, there is now a display of saws, drills, knives, screwdrivers, and other tools.

I looked around the walls of the large room. On the left side, still visible under several coats of paint, were the words *"Haeven Hazot...Shlomo Yeshaya."* Once, when this had been a center of Torah and prayer, there had been a Jew called Shlomo Yeshaya who had made a contribution toward the upkeep of the place, and this was the stone and the inscription commemorating his generosity.

Today, the old Bobover *bet-medrash* is a trade school for girls only. The director, Pan Czisek Tiafel, led me around the room. "I have a surprise for you," he said at last. He walked over to the Eastern wall and drew aside a curtain behind which there was a glass facade that concealed an *aron kodesh*, a holy ark, covered with the red drapery of a *parochet*.

Overcome with emotion, I gave the director a gift for his school. During the war, he told me, the *bet-medrash* had been used as a stable for the horses of the German army. Afterward, it was remodeled and converted into a trade school.

As we walked out of the building, I instinctively raised my hand and placed it over the spot where a *mezuzah* had once been affixed. The director noticed my gesture. Some day, he assured me, when the place is turned into a museum to house Jewish artifacts, a *mezuzah* will once again be placed on the doorpost. During the war, every Jewish article of value, including prayer books, Torah scrolls, silver, and so on, had been collected by the Bishop of Rzeszow, who promised to preserve them in his museum. Later it was discovered that these objects had been claimed by the Vatican and taken to Rome. Nothing was left in Bobowa.

ספר

קדושת ציון

חלק ראשון
על התורה

דברים יקרים אמרים נעימים תוכם רצוף אהבה ויראת ד',
שיצאו מפי קודש הקדשים אדוני אבי מאורן ורבן של ישראל
הרב הגאון הקדוש

מרן בן ציון הלברשטאם זצ"ל הי"ד
האבד"ק באבוב והגליל יע"א

יוצא לאור על ידי בנו

הק' שלמה הלברשטאם
אבד"ק באבוב

❈

ברוקלין, נוא יארק
שנת תשכ"ז

Right: Inscription on the grave
of the Sanzer Tzaddik Reb
Chain Halberstan in Sanz

Above: Mr. Felix Lippman in the
office of the Congregation in
the Latowice Synagogue

On July 4, 1946, **after the local Jews
were accused of ritual murder,** the
townspeople of Kielce, Poland, attacked the 200 Jews of the town, survivors
of a community which numbered
25,000 before the Holocaust, cruelly
murdering 47 men, women and children and wounding 50 others

...לאחר עלילת דם על

Left: The real reason for the
Kielce Program

בפרט גלה כבוד כי נלקח ארון
האלהים לפ"ק
כתר תורה
כבוד קדושת אדונינו מורינו ורבינו
הרב הגאון הקדוש המקובל איש
אלהים נורא אספקלריא
המאירה מנורה הטהורה שר
התורה יחיד בדורו סבא קדישא
מפורסם בכל קצוי ארץ רבן של
בני הגולה עבודתו ותפלתו הי'
מסירת נפש לד' ונפשו דבוק ביוצרו
גמש כחד משרפי מעלה כבוד
קדושת שם תפארתו מרן חיים
בעהמ"ח ספרי דברי חיים בהרב
חסיד מוה ארי' ליבוש זצ"ל
והצבת קודש גאון מוהרש"ל
גאון חכם צבי זצללה"ה ושימש
בכתר הרבנות פה"ק מ"ו שנים ונפטר
בשיבה טובה ניסן י' למב"י שנת
תרל"ו לפ"ק
תנצב"ה

Chapter 31.
THE BOBOVER CHASSIDIM

Following my conversation with Czisek Tiafel, the director of the Bobowa trade school now housed in the building that had once been the *bet- medrash*, I proceeded to the backyard to see for myself where some of the religious artifacts had been buried by the last Jews to leave the town. I stood upon a cement slab, searching in vain for any sign of the rich and intense life that had once been lived there. A Pole approached me. "You are standing over the opening to the Jewish bath," he told me. Beneath my feet, under the cement slab upon which I was standing, was the *mikvah* that had served the Rebbe and his followers. A short distance away, I found the Rebbe's house, now completely remodeled and occupied by strangers.

Even from my childhood, I understood the Bobover chassidim to be a unique group of orthodox Jews, committed not only to observing the laws between man and God, but also assuming an exemplary attitude with respect to their responsibilities toward their fellow man. In the truest sense, it seemed to me then as it does now, that the Bobovers emphasized the basic tenets of *chesed*, of loving-kindness, which is at the root of the word *chassid*, and which is embodied in the central tenets of the philosophy of the Baal Shem Tov, the founder of chassidism.

The first chassidim--the *chassidim rishonim*--are mentioned in the Talmud. Thoroughly devoted to the Torah and its commandments, their only fear was *Morah Shamayim* --fear of God and of sin. They sanctified and purified themselves to better serve God, and performed atonement even for a dubious transgression. According to the Talmud, they would prepare themselves an hour before prayer in order to better concentrate during the service itself (*Brachot* 5a). They would refrain from speaking during prayer, even when danger threatened. They would take pains to bury broken glass and other dangerous objects so that if someone should stumble, he would not be injured (*Tosefta* B.K. 6B).

These early chassidim were also known as *anshei ma'aseh*, men of deeds, in recognition of the good deeds they performed and the miracles they wrought. In their view, a miracle was a natural occurrence, ongoing evidence of God's presence among men. Armed with their faith in God, they had no fear of the Greek occupiers. While Hillel pointed out that an *Am Ha'aretz* could not be considered a chassid (*Avot* 2:5), the credo of these chassidim was, "What's mine is yours, and what's yours is yours" (*Avot* 5:10). Members of this original group of chassidim included Choni Hamagel--Abba Chilkiya--and Chanina Ben Dosa, and the Talmud advises us that the first chassid was Adam himself (*Erubin* 18:B). Reb Pinchas Ben Yair said: "There are many things a person must do to achieve *chassidus*." To reach the high level of a chassid, one had to do more than was expected.

The originator of *chassidism* as we think of it today was Rabbi Yisrael ben Eliezer Baal Shem Tov, who attracted many followers with his emphasis on *Yirat Shamayim* and *Avodat Hashem*, fear of Heaven and serving the Lord. Despite opposition from within the Jewish community itself, and despite persecution from the outside, chassidism quickly spread throughout Poland, Austrian Galicia, the Ukraine, Hungary, and the entire Eastern Europe.

Certain chassidic leaders, among them Rabbi Chaim Ben Leibush Halberstam (1793-1876), known as the Sanzer Tzaddik or the *Divrei Chaim*, took great pains to insist that their disciples not waste their time with involvement in the internecine struggles among the various chassidic sects, but that they devote themselves, instead, to the study of the Torah and the Talmud. "Come to me after your mind has been filled with *Gemara* and *Tosefot*," he declared to his followers. This approach was carried on and reinforced by his son, Rabbi Yechezkel Shragai Halberstam, known as the Shinever Rebbe, the author of *Divrei Yechezkel*..

The grandson, Rabbi Shlomo Ben Reb Meir Nossan (1847-1906) earned distinction as the builder of yeshivot wherever he resided. He was once the rabbi of Oswiecim, but later moved to Bobowa, where he founded a great center of learning with a following of hundreds of students, and established the Bobover dynasty. His son, Rabbi Benzion Halberstam (1873-1941) continued the emphasis on learning, establishing many Etz Chaim yeshivot throughout the length and breadth of Galicia, where thousands of students studied Torah and practiced the Bobover creed of loving-kindness and responsibility for their fellow human beings.

Chapter 32.
THE BOBOVER DYNASTY

After the death of the first Bobover Rebbe, Rabbi Shlomo Ben Meir Nossan Halberstam, his son, Benzion, became the heir to the Bobover "throne." He was thirty-three years old at the time, and he devoted himself to continuing the work of his father, building yeshivot which became centers of Torah learning and fear of God. Thousands of followers would flock to Bobowa, especially for the holidays of *Succot* and *Shavuot*..

Rabbi Benzion Halberstam became known throughout Poland for his wisdom, attracting a host of disciples, and he was especially admired for the beautiful music and melodies that he composed. A Yeshiva Etz Chaim would spring up wherever a Bobover synagogue or *shtibel* was located. Whenever a Bobover student, recommended by the Rebbe, came to a town, he would be welcomed with respect and generous hospitality. The mistress of the household where he would be invited to take his meals would stand over him as he dined and murmur, "*Ess, ess, mein kind, vestu haben koach zu lernen Torah.*" ("Eat, eat, my child, so that you will have strength to learn Torah.") Because the Rebbe was in such great demand, it was often difficult to gain access to him, and a visitor would be obliged to make an appointment with one of the Rebbe's *gabbaim*..

Some time before the Second World War, the Bobover center was moved to Trzebinia, not far from Chrzanow and my own town of Oswiecim. Trzebinia, a relatively unknown town, experienced a remarkable boom upon the arrival of the Rebbe. Even the Poles realized that an important personage had come to their town, for the Rebbe was rumored to be one of the advisors to Marshal Joseph Pilsudsky, the leader of the Polish republic. The Rebbe was popular not only with Jews, but also with Polish officials and police, who acknowledged his wisdom in worldly affairs as well as in Torah .

I remember the day the Rebbe made a visit to our town of Oswiecim. The police prepared carefully for the event, closing off the marketplace for the day, as if in anticipation of the arrival of a head of state. Thousands of chassidim from Oswiecim and the neighboring towns converged on the marketplace, and hundreds of non-Jews also came out to welcome this royal figure.

Suddenly, twelve horses bearing twelve chassidim dressed in red coats appeared, sounding bugles to proclaim the arrival of *Kavod Hod Malchuto*, the leader of the Jewish people, the Bobover Rebbe. Behind the horsemen came a chariot drawn by three pairs of horses. A great cry rose up from the crowd, which began to sing ecstatically, *"Kol rina v'yeshuah b'ohalei tzaddikim"* to welcome the Rebbe. After a while, even the Poles joined in the song: *"Ay vay vishua poyechali zadikim.."*

The procession went on for several hours. People followed the Rebbe's carriage to the main Oswiecim synagogue on Ulica Berka Yoselowicza (*Die Yiddishe Gass*). This synagogue, a short while later destroyed by the Nazis, held several thousand people. The Rebbe delivered his remarks, after which the town leaders officially greeted their distinguished guest. Long afterward, the song, *"Kol Rina,"* remained popular and continued to be sung by everyone. The Rebbe's visit generated great good will between the Jewish and Polish communities of Oswiecim.

This happened over fifty years ago, yet I recall it as if it were only yesterday. I can still see the faces of the Galician Jews, glowing with happiness, on that remarkable day. But then I am overcome by the bitter realization that almost all of those people gathered in the marketplace that day to greet the Bobover Rebbe had been wiped out, and their centers of learning and all their institutions had been decimated. Here and there I come across a few fortunate individuals who had somehow been spared, but, overall, the community had been turned into bone and ash. As I revisit the Oswiecim of my youth, now ignominiously etched in human memory as Auschwitz, I think of the words of the prophet Ezekiel: "Can these bones live?"

And the Lord spoke to Ezekiel: "Behold, O my people, I will open your graves and cause you to rise out of your graves and bring you to the land of Israel." These words of comfort fill my thoughts as I turn from the wasteland of Auschwitz to the vibrant communities of chassidim in Israel and the United States. Once again I hear the laughter of children, and the sound of learning and prayer coming from the yeshivot and the synagogues.

In today's Bobover communities, I see the continuation of the tradition so brutally severed by the Holocaust. Though I am no prophet, I imagine myself privileged to witness the fulfillment of the prophecy of Ezekiel as he stood in the valley of the bones: "There was a noise, a shaking, and the bones came together. Bone to bone, the sinews and flesh upon them, and the skin covered them above...and the breath came into them and they lived and stood up upon their feet--an exceeding great army." Today's vital Bobover chassidim have no need to agonize over continuity or the disaffection of their youth. Through the examples of the parents, and their positive influence upon their children, the Bobover tradition of love of God, love of fellow man, and the study of Torah continues to be instilled in the future generation, and the link between the past and the future continues to be powerfully forged in the present.

Chapter 33.
BOBOVER CHASSIDIM TODAY

My visit to the stark remains of the Bobover community in Poland inspired me to turn, for hope and comfort, to the renewal of Bobover life in Jerusalem, in the central headquarters in Borough Park in the United States, and, in particular, to Kiryat Bobov in Bat Yam, Israel. While the disappearance of the Yiddish language is everywhere decried, in Kiryat Bobov, Yiddish, *Mama Loshen*, is alive and flourishing. In the streets, classrooms, and synagogues of Bat Yam, a robust and fluent Yiddish, as was once spoken in Galicia, can be heard, even from the mouths of children at play. The Bobover chassidim of Bat Yam, with their emphasis on *hemshech*--continuity--are not troubled by the alienation of their children that afflicts so many other Jewish communities. Nor are they affected by the serious problem of emigration from Israel that plagues other parts of the country. On the contrary, aliyah to Israel comes primarily from these religious groups.

The Rebbe's support of the *yishuv* of Kiryat Bobov was ardent and strong from the very beginning. My nephew, Usher Weiss, was studying at the yeshiva in Bat Yam when I first visited the community in 1976. The Rebbe was planning a trip for the Shavuot holiday in order to lend his encouragement to his followers. Hundreds of his chassidim made preparations to accompany him.

The Rebbe's trip was organized by his "foreign minister," Rabbi Moshe Elias, a survivor of the Holocaust whom the Rebbe had brought over to the United States. Rabbi Elias prospered in America, and he never left his benefactor's side. Four hundred chassidim accompanied the Rebbe to Israel, converting the El Al jumbo jet in which they traveled to a flying *bet-medrash* in which they studied and prayed together. The Rebbe quoted Torah during the meals, distributed *shirayim* (the remains of his portion) to his disciples, and even elicited the cooperation of the plane's staff. The other passengers joined the chassidim in the religious services, some for the first time. Bobover chassidim also arrived from Canada and other countries, and, of course, the Bobovers who already resided in Israel converged on Bat Yam for this great occasion. Accommodations were found for everyone; no one dared to say "*Tzar li hamakom*" ("I have no room") in the presence of the Bobover Rebbe.

The Rebbe's visit was a momentous event, drawing together a host of people, with many remarkable stories. One man that I met, a husky chassid with long sidelocks, a survivor of Auschwitz, told me that his job at the death camp had been to shove victims into the gas chambers as SS guards stood by with whips. After the doors were sealed, he had to go to the other side, wait to receive the corpses, and load them onto conveyors to be incinerated in the crematoria.

One day, among the condemned, he spotted the face of Rabbi Sholem Eliezer Halberstam, from Ratzferd, Hungary. Although Rabbi Halberstam's beard and *payot* had been shaven, this chassid recognized him. "Holy Rebbe," he said to Rabbi Halberstam, "you should know that this is your final journey. From here, no one comes out alive."

The Rebbe was not surprised, but as a personal favor, he begged this chassid ("*Ich beit dich*") to bring him a *tallis koton*, a fringed garment. The following morning, the chassid smuggled a kosher *tallis koton* to the Rebbe, who wept and cried, "*Ich bensch dich mit arichas yomim*" ("I bless you with a long life"). Then the Rebbe began to dance with the chassid, thanking God for the opportunity to perform this last *mitzvah* of reciting the blessing over the *tzizit*.

The chassid went on to remind me that while it is well known that the Nazis took pains to exterminate all those who had taken part in the processing of the victims in order that there not be any witnesses, he nevertheless survived. The chassid attributed his survival to Rabbi Sholem Eliezer's blessing of a long life. Among the Rebbe's artifacts, the chassid found the *tallis koton*, which he still had in his possession. His encounter with the Rebbe deepened his faith in God and inspired him to commit himself to a full religious life.

In Bat Yam I also met another individual, a young chassid, about twenty-five years old. He told me that he was a convert, a former university student from Buffalo, New York, with no previous connection to Judaism, a lost soul seeking a new life. Several years earlier, he somehow found his way into a Bobover *bet-medrash*, and he never left. He was converted, took on the new name and, in Kiryat Bobov, he studied *Gemara* and *Tosefot* and was considered a learned man. His Yiddish was fluent, and in every respect, he resembled a typical Bobover chassid.

I gazed at this young man with his blond beard and sidelocks, and as he danced with the other chassidim, I saw his face transformed with exaltation as the Rebbe's eyes met his. The melody that was sung had been composed by the late Bobover Rebbe, Rabbi Benzion Halberstam, who perished in 1941 in Lemberg. The chassidim sang this melody with extraordinary fervor, for this is the song that, according to Bobover tradition, will accompany them when they come out to welcome the Messiah.

Chapter 34.
THE BOBOVER WAY OF LIFE

In 1967 (5727, according to the Jewish calendar), Rabbi Shlomo Halberstam, the present Bobover Rebbe, published *Sefer Kedushat Zion*, a book authored by his father, Rabbi Benzion Halberstam. For this work, the son wrote an introduction, which deals, in particular, with his father's activities in Galicia. In this introduction, the Bobover Rebbe writes: "I have called this book *Sefer Kedushat Zion* in order to remember my father, Benzion, who died *Al Kiddush Hashem* [as a martyr sanctifying God] at the hands of the Germans, may their memory be erased. The book is also in memory of his son, my brother, Moshe Aharon, for the *gematria* [numerical value] of *Kedushat Zion* is *Zichron Livno Moshe Aharon* [a memorial to his son, Moshe Aharon]."

The introduction goes on to describe the wandering, suffering, and murder of his father: "One would require volumes in order to describe what we suffered at the hands of the Nazis up until that bitter and unfortunate day, the fourth of Av, 5701, when my father was killed. My brother, Moshe Aharon and my brother-in-law, were also murdered at the same time. So, too, were Yechezkel Shraga Halberstam, the son of the Czechover Rebbe; Rabbi Moshe Stempel, the son of the well-known Rabbi Feivish Stempel of Krakow; and Rabbi Shlomo Rubin, the son of Rabbi Tzvi Hirsch from Mishlenitz. My brother, Chaim Yehoshua, was caught in Lvov and deported by the Russians to Siberia, where he perished in prison. The only ones who remained alive, by the grace of God, were my mother, my sisters, one of my brothers, Rabbi Yechezkel David, and I."

According to the Rebbe, not only was *Sefer Kedushat Zion* published in memory of his father, Benzion, but the Bobover yeshiva, B'nai Zion, was also established to commemorate the life of this great leader. Because the Rebbe was killed and had no burial place, this book and this yeshiva would have to serve as his monument. Studying the words of Torah contained in *Sefer Kedushat Zion*, is, for me, like a visit to the monument (*zion*) of the Bobover Rebbe, who inspired me in my childhood when I visited his large *shop*, or hall, in Trzebinia, and who raised my spirit with his prayers, his sweet voice, and the wonderful melodies he composed.

Sefer Kedushat Zion was dedicated by the son, Rabbi Shlomo Halberstam, to the young chassidim who had never known his father, Benzion. Through the commentary on the Five Books of Moses, Rabbi Shlomo Halberstam sought to draw future generations to the luminous personality of his father. In this work, Rabbi Benzion Halberstam stressed the three pillars upon which the world rests--Torah, *Avodah* (service), and *Gemilut Chassadim* (acts of loving-kindness).

The emphasis on Torah was apparent immediately upon the succession of Rabbi Benzion Halberstam to the position of his father, Rabbi Shlomo Halberstam, the first Bobover Rebbe. As leader of the great yeshiva in Bobov, Rabbi Benzion Halberstam gave personal attention to each student, frequently sitting for hours with a particular young man, who would leave the Rebbe's chamber with his spirit refreshed and his soul uplifted.

The student would often confess his sins to the Rebbe and ask to be shown how to repent. The Rebbe would warn against fasting and mortification of the flesh as a method of atonement. "They bring a person to sadness and depression," he would say, "and this is not the way of Torah or chassidus." Instead, the Rebbe would suggest that the student involve himself more intensively in Torah study, and do so with rejoicing: *Ivdu es HaShem b'simcha, bouh lefonov birnana*; serve God with happiness, come before Him with gladness.

The establishment of the first Etz Chaim Bobover yeshiva soon after World War I was followed by the opening of many others throughout Galicia to accommodate the thousands of students who chose the Bobover way of education and of life. The Rebbe was careful to engage the best teachers, imbued with Torah and fear of God. When Polish zlotys plummeted in value, the Rebbe paid the teachers in dollars. Bobover yeshivot became the centers of Torah learning and the chassidic way of life in Galician Poland.

For Rabbi Benzion Halberstam, service to God was carried out and enhanced through his musical gifts. He had a beautiful singing voice, and he composed many lovely melodies to fit the words of the prayers. As he prayed for himself, his household, and the entire congregation of Israel, like the priests in the Temple, he would be overcome with emotion and his eyes would fill with tears. His royal table (*tisch*) was conducted with sanctity and generosity, drawing around it thousands of chassidim. The *zmirot* that he sang, the insights into the Torah that he uttered, and the stories that he told of the great t*zaddikim*, served as an inspiration to everyone present, and often led his followers to greater and more heartfelt adherence to the Torah way of life.

The Bobover Rebbe's acts of loving-kindness were emblemized in his *tzedakah*, his charity. His heart and hand were always open to the poor, to brides seeking a dowry, and to representatives of Torah institutions in Poland and in Israel. In particular, Rabbi Benzion Halberstam attended to the personal needs of his students, many of whom were poor and came from impoverished families. When a prosperous member of the community would suffer a serious financial loss, the Rebbe would help him get back on his feet, taking pains to spare him embarrassment of any sort.

The Bobover way of life, based on Torah, *Avodah*, and *Gemilut Chassadim* had been instilled in me by my parents from my childhood. It has served as the inspiration of my youth, and continues to evoke in me a love for chassidism and a desire to aspire to the lofty standards of learning, behavior, and spiritual dedication as exemplified by the Bobover Rebbe.

Chapter 35.
THE RABBI'S SON AS AN SS OFFICER

"I'm not certain if he was a Bobover, Belzer, or Radomsker chassid,"
said my guide, Yossel Berger, "but he was definitely a chassid. He was
fortunate in that he had an Irish face, with small, sharp eyes, and full,
ruddy cheeks. His gaze resembled the headlights of a car, and he had a
stern, severe look. He wore his SS uniform as neatly as any German. I
met him in the Plaszow extermination camp where he was able--this
'chassid'--to move with ease in and out of the camp, coming and going
as he pleased. He helped as many people as he was able, and often,
without a word, he would wipe the tears off an inmate's face and give
him an extra piece of bread. He was the kindest SS man I had ever
encountered, and I have encountered many.

"After the war, I visited Sanz, and there he was, dressed in civilian
clothes. It was then that he informed me that he had been a chassid before
the war. He told me that he had been caught giving a piece of bread to
a Jewish prisoner in Plaszow. He had escaped a day before his trial and
had wandered as a civilian until the war ended."

While this story, on the face of it, seemed unbelievable, in Miami,
Florida I met a gentleman from Toronto with a similar tale. Amnon
Aizenstadt is the son of the Rebbe of Tzozmir, known as Sandomierz
in Polish. He claims to be the only rabbi's son to have successfully
infiltrated the SS and remain alive. Yossel Berger's story, of course,
suggested that there may have been others as well who had survived in
this astonishing way.

During the war, Amnon Aizenstadt, who to this very day resembles an Aryan, was known as Adam Arendarsky. He was twenty-three years old when the Nazis rounded up the Jews of his city. His Aryan features enabled him to escape the fate of his brothers, and he has written two books recounting his experiences as an SS officer in the Warsaw Ghetto, and as a foreman in a factory operated by the Germans. The first book, written in Yiddish, is called, *The Earth Did Not Cover the Blood*, and the second, in English, is entitled, *Chronicles of Jewish Resistance*. (Mosaic Press, Oakville, Canada)

The two works, which he presented to me, recount his background as the son of the Tzozmirer Rebbe and the descendant of a long line of *tzaddikim*.. His gentile appearance, as well as his knowledge of German, Polish, and Russian, enabled him to survive as he traveled through Krakow, posing as an Aryan. When it was discovered that he was helping Jews, he fled to a small town to escape punishment by the Nazis. There he met a German who recognized him as a capable manager, and offered him the job of recruiting workers for the *Luftwaffe* in German-occupied Russia.

This German, an officer in the Luftwaffe himself, provided Amnon with the proper official documents and outfitted him with an SS uniform. As Adam Arendarsky, Amnon appeared in the Warsaw Ghetto dressed in this uniform. He ordered a German soldier to cease harming a Jewish girl, he helped many Jews secure extra ration cards, and he had no problem directing the Jews across the border into Russia. According to Amnon Aizenstadt, the Germans never stopped those Jews who wanted to move eastward to Russia, but movement back into Poland was impossible. Amnon Aizenstadt, this SS officer with the gentle Jewish heart, refers to himself as a modern-day Marrano.

Such stories, as incredible as they may seem, truly happened, for those were incredible times. Many survivors emerged from the Holocaust with amazing tales, and many emerged suffering deep psychological and spiritual wounds. According to a Bobover chassid, even the Rebbe had to strengthen himself to escape the depression that overcame him as a result of the many grievous losses he had suffered. For a while, he could not even sing. But his faith in God, and his faith in the perpetuation of the Bobover way of life sustained him. This Bobover chassid remembers how the Rebbe comforted his followers, stressing the importance of prayer and of rejoicing with song. The Rebbe said, "Singing for the sake of singing is artificial, and has little value as prayer. However, when a Jewish soul is filled with Torah and fear of God, the singing and the prayers reach the heights."

Today, the singing of the Bobover chassidim can be heard in their flourishing centers in the United States and in Israel, and though nothing can make up for the devastating losses that had been suffered, the revival of these communities is a profound source of comfort, hope, and rejoicing.

Chapter 36.
ON THE ROAD TO SANZ

From Bobowa we traveled south, passing such small towns as Wilczyska and Stroze. When we reached the intersection of Grybow, we turned right on Route 98 leading to Nowy Sacz (Sanz), the home of the Sanzer Rebbe, author of *Divrei Chaim*. Two villages, Dabrowka Polska and Birgomice divide Nowy Sacz (New Sanz) from Stary Sacz (Old Sanz). The current map shows this town to be only twenty miles from the Czech border to the south.

New Sanz is situated in the province of Krakow in southern Poland. Jewish settlements are known to have existed there as early as 1469, and a Jewish doctor called Abraham practiced in Sanz in 1503. Jews are credited with helping in the rebuilding of Sanz after the Swedish invasion. In 1746, a great synagogue was erected in Sanz, adorned with outstanding frescoes. By 1765, there were more than 600 Jews living in the town in seventy houses. Another 600 Jews resided in the small villages surrounding Sanz.

After Austria annexed the entire area of Galicia in 1772, Sanz became a part of Austria and remained so until after the First World War. At the beginning of the nineteenth century, the Austrians forced the Jews of Sanz into a ghetto. Sanz became a center of chassidic life by the end of the century.

By 1880, there were 5,000 Jews in Sanz, constituting 46 percent of the population of the town. They earned their livelihood selling agricultural products and wood, manufacturing and selling clothing, and working as tailors, carpenters, shoemakers, and engravers. In 1890, the Jewish population of Sanz decreased to 4,100, about 32 percent of the total population of the town. By 1910, there were 8,000 Jews in Sanz, and eleven years later, in 1921, the Jewish residents of Sanz totalled 9,000. In the period between 1900 and 1914, a Jewish school, endowed by the Baron de Hirsch fund, was established in the town, with an enrollment of over 200 students. There were many synagogues, smaller houses of prayer, schools, culture and sports centers supported by the Jewish community of Sanz. On September 1, 1939, when Germany invaded Poland, 10,000 Jews lived in Sanz, with another 5,000 in the neighboring villages.

The Nazis entered Sanz on September 5, 1939. Soon after, 700 Jews from Lodz were resettled in the town, and in August, 1941, all the Jews of Sanz and the surrounding areas were incarcerated in the ghetto. Between 1940 and 1942, several forced labor camps were created in Roznow and other nearby towns. One such camp, Lipie, was in operation from 1942 until 1943, when over 1,000 Jewish prisoners were killed. A Jewish underground was caught by the Germans and its members were executed in the Jewish cemetery of Sanz. During the four days between August 24 and August 28, 1942, the entire Jewish community of Sanz was deported to the Belzec death camp and exterminated.

A heavy rain was falling over Sanz when we reached the outskirts of the town. The rain continued to pour down for several hours as we made our way to the Jewish cemetery. The gates were locked, and we were told that Mrs. Holzer, who lived in the town, had the keys and was the only person with the authority to open the gates. However, because of the downpour, we could not travel any further. About one hundred yards from the cemetery gate I noticed a farm house, and I suggested to my driver that we seek shelter there. A woman close to seventy years in age opened the door, and after we explained the reason for our visit in the area, she invited us inside.

Her name was Anna Krul, she said. "*Ya jestem Anna Krul.*" She had lived at this address, Ulica Rybacka 8, all of her life, she explained. She led us up to the second floor of her home, and directed us to a window overlooking the cemetery. This cemetery is the resting place of many great rabbis, *tzaddikim*, and chassidim--scholars, leaders, and righteous men whose renown extended well beyond the Polish community to the world at large.

Through the window of Anna Krul's house, I was able to see many monuments, some erect, some half sunk in the ground. Stone slabs engraved with names and epitaphs stood in one corner. These tombstones had been reclaimed by Jews who returned after the war and pried them out of sidewalks, stairwells, and walls, where the Germans had used them for their construction projects. Mrs. Krul noticed my interest. "From this window I have seen the most horrible things," she said. I pleaded with her to tell me. Though she refused at first, a little coaxing and a gift of a few dollars persuaded her to relate her story.

Chapter 37.
THE MASS GRAVE AT SANZ

Anna Krul was born after the First World War and had lived all of her life in the two-story farm house set on two acres of land adjacent to the Jewish cemetery of Sanz. Hers had been an isolated life. Few visitors came to her door, and fear of strangers had been imbued in her over her almost seventy years. But with the new liberalization in Poland, and reassured that we meant her no harm, she began to open up with her story, though throughout the telling, her head turned from side to side and her eyes darted here and there, for nothing could fully erase a lifetime of terror.

When the Nazis came to Sanz in early September, 1939, Mrs. Krul told us, they broke down the gates of the cemetery, entered, and began to throw down the monuments. They also moved in on her farm house with the intention of destroying it, but for some reason changed their mind. Because she was a young and attractive woman at the time, her mother locked her in the attic to save her from the attentions of the German ruffians. From her small attic window, she watched them demolish the monuments in the cemetery and destroy the small house that stood where the holy rabbi of Sanz had been buried.

In 1942, Mrs. Krul recalled, just before the Jews were deported from Nowy Sacz to be murdered, truckloads of young boys were brought to the cemetery, about 200 young men in all. They were given shovels and ordered to dig. Anna Krul watched as these innocent young men dug a ditch about 200 feet in length. In the late afternoon, the Germans lined up the men at the edge of the ditch, ordered them to stand at attention, and shot them in the back of the neck. Within minutes, all 200 fell into the ditch, dead.

The next morning, said Mrs. Krul, she again observed trucks arriving at the cemetery, this time bearing about 200 young women. They, too, were ordered to stand at attention, and they, too, were shot in the back of the neck, and, one by one, fell into the ditch. Several hours later, workers were brought in to cover up the mass grave. Then the Germans arrived and loaded monuments and tombstones into trucks and drove them away. The memory of what she had witnessed, said Mrs. Krul, haunts her to this day.

Anna Krul offered to take me into the cemetery through a secret entrance, but because of the inclement weather, I declined her invitation. However, she did give me the address of Mrs. Holzer, who had the key to cemetery, and when the rain stopped we made our way to the Mrs. Holzer's home in the *Rynek*, the main square of Sanz.

I remembered Mrs. Holzer from my first visit. She was a widow, a gentile who had been married to a Jew and who had never converted. Authority over the cemetery was passed down to her from her late husband, who, in addition to overseeing the burial site, also took care of the small synagogue in Sanz. Mrs. Holzer has two children with beautiful Jewish faces. Her son is the one who maintains the cemetery, and it was he who led us there and unlocked the gate. Inside the cemetery, I found the grave of Rabbi Chaim Ring. I recited some chapters of *Tehilim*.

There is only one Jew living in Sanz today, Mrs. Regina (Rivka) Kempinska, 69 years old. She lives with her daughter and gentile son-in-law on a small side street on the outskirts of the town, which is rather difficult to find, at Ulica Pygonia 22 (telephone: 23529).

Mrs. Kempinska is ailing and spends most of her time in bed. She tries to speak Hebrew, and her Yiddish is good. Our conversation was in a mixture of Yiddish, Hebrew, and Polish. She told me that she has a brother-in-law, Dov Kempinsky, who lives in Rishon LeZion, in Israel, as well as a cousin, Marcel Riegelhaupt, whose address she could not recall. Later on, I succeeded in finding her relatives for her. She told me that many of them had shortened their name to Kemp.

Regina Kempinska was 19 years old when the war started. She already had a good general and Jewish education. She was active in the Polish underground at the beginning of the war, and was able to pass as a Polish woman. But she was soon caught, because, as she put it, she "knew too much." She succeeded in fleeing to the forest after her arrest, where she married a young man and became pregnant. Her life in those days was extremely difficult. She was constantly forced to move from place to place, and she was arrested eight times, she said, but on each occasion managed to escape.

"All my friends urged me to have an abortion," said Regina Kempinska, "but I refused." In 1942, she gave birth to a daughter in a forest under a pine tree. After that, she was never caught again, but wandered from place to place with her child, hiding in the homes of gentiles. When the war ended, she settled in a town near Sanz.

Regina Kempinska's daughter and son-in-law expressed to me a great eagerness to settle in Israel. The daughter's husband indicated a longing to convert to Judaism. I gave him the names and addresses of some orthodox rabbis, explaining to him that if his conversion were carried out in accordance with *halacha*, he and his wife would certainly find no trouble making a home in Israel and feeling comfortable there.

Chapter 38.
REB CHAIM RING OF SANZ

The town of Nowy Sacz, or, in Yiddish, Sanz, in southern Galicia was
once a great center of Torah and chassidic life. The *gaon* and *tzaddik*,
Rabbi Chaim Halberstam, dominated the spiritual life there. He was the
author of *Divrei Chaim*, a major work that consists of three volumes.
The first book discusses the laws of divorce, the second is a collection
of responsa on many subjects, and the third contains *drashot* on the
weekly Torah portion.

Rabbi Chaim Halberstam was born in 1793 in Tarnograad. He was
descended, on his mother's side, from the author of the *Chacham Tzvi*.
His illustrious teachers were the Chozeh of Lublin, Rabbi Naftali of
Ropshitz, and Rabbi Tzvi Hirsch of Zidichov. Rabbi Chaim Halberstam
studied together with Rabbi Yisrael of Rizhin, the Belzer Rebbe Shalom
Rokeach, and Rabbi Tzvi Hirsch of Rimanov.

About one hundred years ago, the great "battle" between the
Sanzer and the Sadgur chassidim was in full swing. Nobody would have
imagined then that, many years later, a Sadgur chassid, Reb Chaim
Ring, the only remaining Jew in Sanz, would take upon himself the
responsibility of keeping a watchful eye over the grave of the Sanzer
Tzaddik, Rabbi Chaim Halberstam. I met Reb Chaim when he was 74
years old, tall, thin, and in good health. He always walked with a cane
in his hand.

My first meeting with Reb Chaim Ring took place in Sanz, in the
home of Mr. and Mrs. Leibshard. At the time, there were twelve Jewish

families living in Sanz. Mr. Leibshard, who was one of those rare Jews who returned to his home town after the war hoping for the best and actually remained, was the community leader of this small group. Now he was preparing to emigrate to Israel with his wife and sixteen year old daughter. He was leaving primarily for his daughter's sake, because of his concern that she was growing up without any Jewish friends. As soon as I returned to the United States after that first trip to Poland, I found a pen pal for the Leibshards' daughter. Devorah Leibshard wrote in Polish, and the sixteen-year-old American girl from Yeshiva University High School for Girls with whom I had put her in touch answered in Yiddish. It was truly astonishing how much these two young Jewish women had in common.

When I asked Reb Chaim Ring during that visit at the Leibshard home why he chose to remain in Poland when the doors of Israel and the United States were open to him, he replied that he was an old man and there was nothing left for him to do but watch over the monument of the Sanzer Tzaddik.. And when I cautioned him that the Poles might try to harm him, the feisty old man declared, "*Mit mein shtecken vel ich zey derlangen, die anti-Semiten!*" ("I will beat those anti-Semites with my stick!") Then I understood why he always carried a cane.

At first, Reb Chaim Ring did not talk much, but when the name of the Sanzer Tzaddik was mentioned his face lit up. He remembered my grandfather, Reb Anschel, whom he had known well. My grandfather had grown up in Sanz and later became the *gabbai* of the *Divrei Yechezkel* in Shineve. "Do you know how many Jews used to come to Sanz for the 'Third Day of Pesach?'" Reb Chaim Ring began. "The twenty-fifth of Nissan, three days after Pesach, was the *yahrzeit* of the death of the Sanzer Tzaddik, and, without exaggeration, thousands of people came from all over Galicia and Poland. The town burst with life. The chassidim used to call the Sanzer *yahrzeit* 'The Third Day of Pesach,' or the '*Hillula*..'"

A few visitors continued to come to visit the grave of the Sanzer Tzaddik even after the war, Reb Chaim went on to tell me, particularly from Krakow and the vicinity, but later, hardly anyone arrived for the *yahrzeit*. Recently, however, some chassidim have come from Europe and the United States. Only Reb Chaim Ring faithfully visited the cemetery every day. He would open the gate, enter the enclosure where the Tzaddik and his family were interred, and spend several hours reciting *Tehilim*. He told me that he had been beaten by thugs several times, but even so, he never faltered in his mission.

In Sanz today, the visitor can find patches in the sidewalk that mark the places where the Germans had installed monuments from the Jewish cemetery. These monuments were brought back to the burial ground by returning Jews after the war, but occasionally one can still spot a Jewish epitaph face up in the street. Polish anti-Semitism persisted in Sanz after the war to such a degree that a request by Jewish residents to carry guns in order to protect themselves was granted by the authorities. Reb Chaim Ring told me that, on occasion, these weapons had to be used by Jews to defend themselves against attacks by Polish hoodlums.

Reb Chaim Ring was truly an inspiring presence, for here was a man who was prepared to sacrifice himself for an ideal--the ideal of overseeing the grave of the Sanzer Tzaddik. But there was one question I could not help asking myself: Who would watch over Reb Chaim Ring?

Chapter 39.
THE TWO MONUMENTS OF THE SANZER
TZADDIK

The more I came to know Reb Chaim Ring, the more I grew to admire him. As our friendship developed, he described to me how he had made the transition from a Sadgur to a Sanzer chassid. At first, he sought to understand, through study and research, the sources of the rivalry between the Sanzer and the Sadgur chassidim. As part of this process, he studied the *Divrei Chaim* of the Sanzer Tzaddik, and so taken was he by this masterful work, and, in particular, by the Tzaddik's acknowledgement, through citations and references, of the great thinkers and teachers who had preceded him, that Reb Chaim Ring decided that he would become a Sanzer chassid.

It often happens that a scholar forgets where he derived his thoughts and naturally assumes that all of them originated with him. Not so the Sanzer Tzaddik, Rabbi Chaim Halberstam. In his *Divrei Chaim*, he quotes Rambam, Ramban, the *Kuzari* of Yehuda HaLevi, Avraham ibn David, Rabbi Yeshaya Horowitz, the Maharal, and even the *Siddur* of Rabbi Yaakov Emden. A scholar's true depth can be recognized in his generous willingness to acknowledge and draw from the work of those who preceded him.

Rabbi Chaim Halberstam, the Sanzer Tzaddik, is recognized as one of the first masters who insisted that the chassidism of the Baal Shem Tov was not, in and of itself, a sufficient goal. The Baal Shem emphasized two elements. First, that the presence of God is everywhere, in every object and every being, a fact that each individual is required to keep in mind always in order to better serve God. The second element is derived from the *Kabalah*, where it is taught that the physical world and the divine world have a constant, complementary effect and influence on each other, so that even daily human needs are part of serving God. The main goal of a chassid, the Baal Shem taught, is devotion to God in order to bring man closer to the divine presence. Such devotion could be achieved through prayer, but it must be sincere, fervent prayer. In the early days of chassidism, the study of Torah for its own sake was not emphasized; rather, such study was valued only when it led to deeds. The Sanzer Tzaddik, on the other hand, insisted that the genuine chassid must first prepare himself through the study of Torah. He would urge his disciples not to waste their youths coming to him until they had filled their heads with *Gemara* and *Tosefot*..

These and similar analyses of chassidic philosophy filled my conversation with Reb Chaim Ring. I was overwhelmed with admiration for this unusual man and amazed to find such an individual in modern-day Poland. Then I posed a question to him that had been troubling me ever since my visit to the Jewish cemetery. "Why are there two identical tombstones for the Sanzer Tzaddik?" I asked Reb Chaim. "That is a truly remarkable story," he replied, and he invited me to his one-room apartment where he offered me a hot drink and began his tale.

Immediately after the war, Reb Chaim told me, many Jews attempted to return to Sanz from Russia and reclaim their homes, which were now occupied by Poles. There was a pogrom in which a number of Jews were hurt, but they persisted nevertheless. One of their very first acts upon their return to the town was to go to the cemetery and pray at the grave of the Sanzer Tzaddik.. There, to their horror, they found almost total devastation. The Rebbe's enclosure and all the stones it once contained had disappeared. There had been at least ten other *tzaddikim* buried there, a *minyan*, including two of the Rebbe's seven sons, Rabbi Meir Nosson, the father of the Bobover dynasty who had died young, 21 years before his father in 1876, and Rabbi Aharon, the *Krazer Rav*, whom the Tzaddik had appointed rabbi of Sanz in his own lifetime. Also buried there was the Sanzer Tzaddik's son-in-law, Reb Yitzchak Tovia Rubin, husband of the Rebbe's eldest daughter by his second marriage, Nechomele. In addition to these distinguished leaders, there were also grandchildren, all of whom were important personalities and righteous men.

The first group of returning Jews decided to replace the Rebbe's monument. Measuring the cemetery from all four corners, they finally arrived at a consensus as to exactly where the enclosure had once stood and precisely where the Tzaddik's resting place had been. They also had a clear picture of the tombstone from a photograph that one of the Jews always carried around with him. They proceeded to order a stone, which was engraved with exactly the same epitaph that had been on the original, and which they erected on the designated spot.

Soon after, another group of Jews returned to Sanz, not only from Russia this time, but from many other cities in Galicia. When they arrived at the cemetery to pray at the grave of the Sanzer Tzaddik, they declared that the stone had been placed on the wrong spot. They, too, measured and calculated, and they came to the conclusion that the correct site was three graves away from where the present monument stood. The Sanzer chassidim sent messages to rabbis to help resolve this dilemma, and it was decreed that a new tombstone be erected on the new and correct spot. On the base of the first monument a sign was placed: "This is not the grave of Rabbi Chaim Sanzer, but of other *tzaddikim.*" "And so," concluded Reb Chaim Ring, "this is why you see two monuments for one man, the Sanzer Tzaddik, Rabbi Chaim Halberstam.

Reb Chaim Ring went on to tell me that soon after these events, two wealthy Jews from England came and erected an enclosure for the graves. Thus, the *minyan* of the great *tzaddikim* can once again be found under a single roof.

Today, the visitor to the Jewish cemetery of Sanz will also find the gravestone of Reb Chaim Ring, who had devoted his life to watching over the resting place of the Sanzer Tzaddik.

Chapter 40.
KATOWICE

My three-hour journey from Warsaw to Katowice was made in the company of three Polish men: Josef Mach, the representative of an organization attempting to improve Polish-Israeli relations in the name of Janusz Korczak, whose office in Katowice is decorated with Jewish and Israeli pictures and symbols; Marian Jurowicz, president of the Katowice soccer team, who is trying to organize a game between Maccabee Tel Aviv and the Polish team; and Zygmunt Staczira, commissioner of the Polish soccer organization. From these traveling companions I learned that HaPoel of Tel Aviv, which has two Polish members, would be arriving to play in Poland, and that this event would be followed by a match between the two teams in Tel Aviv.

Josef Mach also informed me that new Polish laws are now making it easier for Jews to reclaim property confiscated during the war, particularly such public Jewish properties as synagogues, schools, and community centers. In Mr. Mach's opinion, a good deal of Polish real estate rightfully belongs to Jews, and he suggested that wealthy Jews organize a foundation to fund legal action to reclaim this lost property.

In Katowice, I was a guest at the home of Mr. Shrage Feivel ben Moshe HaCohen (Felix) Lippman. Mr. Lippman told me that he was born in Wodzislaw, a town whose population was 90 percent Jewish. Mr. Lippman remained in Wodzislaw until war broke out in 1939. After the war, in 1946, Mr. Lippman was among the 200 Jews who returned to Kielce, a neighboring town, where he was an eyewitness to the infamous Kielce pogrom.

There are many accounts of the Kielce pogrom, which took place on July 4, 1946, and in which 42 people were killed. According to one version, the pogrom was precipitated by the return of the Jews to the town and their attempt to reclaim their property from the Poles. Another account attributes the murder of the 42 to the resentment of the Polish nationalists, in collusion with the Polish communists, over the attempt of the Jews to reorganize their community upon their return to Kielce from Russia, the camps, and various hiding places. The police, too, were said to have been implicated in the action, for on the day before the pogrom, they searched Jewish homes and confiscated whatever weapons they could find.

Mr. Lippman's account threw an entirely new light on the event. According to Mr. Lippman, several hundred Jews from all over had come to Kielce to settle there. A Polish anti-Semitic nationalistic organization wanted to liquidate the existing communist party in Kielce, and decided to use the Jews to provoke a revolt. A rumor was spread that a Christian child had been kidnapped and killed by Jews for their religious rituals. On the morning of July 4, 1946, thousands of people began to run to a street called "Planty," where they surrounded a house inhabited by Jews. Shots rang out, and by the end of the day, 42 Jews had been killed and many others wounded.

All of this information was brought out in the ensuing trial, Mr. Lippman said. The pogrom had nothing to do with taking back Jewish property, he asserted, or with re-establishing Jewish institutions. It was simply another ugly manifestation of ancient forms of anti-Semitism. "Not so long ago," Mr. Lippman went on, "a *pomnik* (monument) was erected in honor of the 42 who had been slain, and their story was told. My daughter, Lea, was present at the ceremony." Lea Lippman is a twenty-year-old college student who is extremely eager to pursue her studies of her Jewish heritage. She handed me a brochure in which she describes herself as "Lea Lippman, Foreign Contacts Bureau in Katowice, Poland." The brochure is printed in English and in Hebrew, indeed a novelty in Poland.

Mr. Lippman took me to the Katowice synagogue. He informed me that there is a *minyan* every Saturday, and on holidays a minimum of twenty people always attend. He was deeply concerned about the wellbeing of the existing Katowice Jewish community. He described their plans to restore the cemetery by putting up a fence and replacing a hundred stones that had been broken or destroyed. They also planned to build a house for the cemetery's caretaker. The estimated cost for all of these projects was $50,000.

When Jews from the United States, Israel, and Australia arrived in Katowice for the ceremony marking the unveiling of a monument on the spot where the main synagogue once stood, they pledged to raise the necessary funds for the restoration of the cemetery. Rabbi Besser from the United States and Mr. Kanarek of Australia did send some money, but it was hardly sufficient to cover the costs. The chairperson of the restoration project is Celia Kartiel of Tel Aviv, who insisted that the monuments be erected first and then the caretaker's house be built. Mr. Lippman argued, in turn, that the restored monuments would be vandalized if there is no caretaker to watch over them.

The remaining Jews in Poland are often so poor that they must turn for assistance to their more fortunate brothers and sisters in other countries. The restoration of whatever is left of Jewish life in Poland is a most worthy cause, for not only must services be provided and maintained for the Jews who are still there, but, in addition, for the sake of memory, there must be as many reminders as possible of the great and vibrant Jewish world that once, before it was so violently annihilated, had flourished in Poland.

Chapter 41.
THE KATOWICE DISTRICT

There are still a few elderly Jews living in the small towns and villages surrounding Katowice. I visited these towns--Sosnowiec, Bedzin, Zawiercie, Gliwice, Bytom, and Zabrze--in the company of Mr. Lippman.

There is no Jewish community any longer in **Sosnowiec**. One year, I found seven Jews in the town, and a year later, if one does not count two who had converted to Catholicism, there were only two remaining Jews--Mr. Rosenzweig and an old woman. Three Jewish cemeteries still stand in the town, which a wealthy American Jew has promised to maintain. Before the war, Sosnowiec was a thriving community, with a population of 28,000 Jews. It was the home of the Radomsker Rebbe. During the war, Jews from Oswiecim, including my sister and her family, were brought to Sosnowiec, and from there were sent back to Oswiecim/Auschwitz, where they all perished.

In **Bedzin**, or Bendin, which once had 25,000 Jews, 50 percent of the total population of the town, only one Jew remains, Mr. Schwartz. No ghetto was ever established in Bedzin or in Sosnowiec during the war; Jews from the neighboring areas were simply collected in these larger towns and then sent to Auschwitz. Immediately after the war, about 150 Jews returned to Bedzin, but the attempt to revive the town never succeeded.

Only one Jew, Mr. Pinchewsky, an eighty-year-old man who cares for his blind, gentile wife, remains in **Zawiercie**. He lives there in great poverty, and I was asked to obtain some assistance for him. Seven thousand Jews resided in Zawiercie before the war. Of this group, about 2,000 anticipated the coming catastrophe and fled before the Germans entered the town. When the Nazis arrived, they ordered all the Jews between the ages of seventeen and fifty to gather in the marketplace in the center of town. These Jews were arrested, tortured for nine days, and eventually transported to Auschwitz, where they perished. The community never revived.

Shmuel Farber is the community leader in **Gliwice**. They have a small, twelve by fifteen foot room, in which weekly Sabbath services are held, attended, according to Mr. Farber, by fifteen men and thirty women. There is always a *kiddush* after the prayers. Mr. Farber and his assistant work out of a small room adjacent to the synagogue. There are eighty Jews in Gliwice, but only Mssrs. Gemalinsky, Shirk, Parnes, Sender, Nechwesky, Zacharchyk, and Inkindinker are married to Jewish women. There are two cemeteries, one in good order and the other completely neglected. At the cemetery there is a monument to 78 Jews who had been killed by the Nazis and buried by the cemetery watchman in a mass grave.

In a private conversation, Mr. Farber revealed his despair. "We are a *kehilla* of old and lonely people," he told me. "We used to travel to Katowice daily for a kosher meal, but for some reason, the kosher kitchen has closed down." Anti-Semitism is a daily affliction, Mr. Farber continued. In Lvov, a Jew was tortured to death and his wife beaten. In neighboring Rzabne, vandals destroyed many monuments in the cemetery, and threw garbage in it. A similar thing happened in Lublin, Mr. Farber said. In Szczecin, the name of the main street, which had been called *Bohaterow Ghetto*, or Ghetto Fighters, had been changed.

Mr. Farber gave me the name of two destitute Gliwice Jews who need help. I left him some *tallesim* and *mezuzot*, as well as a *machzor* for Passover, which he requested, so that services could be led properly. Mr. Farber also added that the roof of the main synagogue is in need of repair.

My most recent visit to **Bytom** (Boyton) afforded me with additional information about the remnants of the Jewish community there. Of the forty Jews now residing in Bytom, only two are married to Jewish spouses, Mr. Haber and Mr. Akselrad. Services are held in their *shtibel* on high holidays and on *yahrzeit* days. Mr. Weisenfeld is the president of the synagogue, and Mr. Akselrad is the community leader. Mr. Akselrad informed me that the Jewish community of Bytom consists of thirty men and ten women. There is no one in the town who can read the Torah. Mr. Akselrad's own personal dream of finding a Jewish bride for his son had been fulfilled, he told me. His daughter-in-law is a Russian Jewish woman, and the young couple is planning to emigrate to Israel.

Mrs. Helen Biener, nee Sperling, the secretary of the Bytom Jewish community, related her story to me. She was born in Lemberg (Lvov) in 1910. In 1939, they were driven to Siberia by the Russians. She had only one pair of shoes in which she walked to Siberia. Her feet were frozen when she arrived there after the winter. She was able to remove only one shoe; with the other, her foot came off. She returned to Poland on April 19, 1946, but because of the loss of her foot, she was too ashamed to go back to her hometown of Lvov and went on instead to Bytom where she remained.

"What can I tell you, Rabbiner," Mrs. Biener said to me. "My life has not been a happy one. My father was murdered when I was ten months old. We were a rich family, and my father lent money to people, and one time, when a man came to return money, thieves came as well and murdered my father. My mother remarried. She died when I was eighteen."

I gave Mrs. Biener a *mezuzah*, which I affixed to her door. She began to cry. With great emotion, she walked over to the *mezuzah* on her crutches and kissed it. "I have not had a *mezuzah* since I left Lemberg," she said.

"What about your community?" I asked her. "What can I say? *Es halt schoin by neilah*. People die or leave and are not replaced. My husband is very sick in the chronic-care hospital."

At the conclusion of this interview, which was conducted in the presence of Mr. Akselrad in Yiddish, Polish, and even a little Hebrew, I offered to help Mrs. Biener in any way I could, but she refused all assistance. After parting from this afflicted woman, I went to recite a *Molei* for the 39 Dutch Jews who had been murdered and buried in Bytom.

There are seven Jewish residents of **Zabrze**, including Mr. Farber, the community leader of Gliwice. Zabrze, or, as the Germans called it, Hindenberg, once had a Jewish population of a thousand souls. Because of its proximity to Bytom, many of its Jews were part of the Bytom *kehilla* until they built a synagogue of their own. Michal Boym and Czeslaw Zacharczyk are two of Zabrze's Jews.

Chapter 42.
SOME STATISTICS ON PRESENT-DAY POLISH JEWRY

Upon our return from our discouraging tour of of the Katowice district, Mr. Lippman and I sat down for a serious conversation. Since he is a respected community leader and knowledgeable about the state of Jewish life in Poland, I asked him to describe to me in a forthright manner the precise population statistics for present-day Polish Jewry, as well as to provide me with exact details about the services available to the pitiful remnants of what had once been a flourishing community.

Mr. Lippman asserted, first of all, that the Warsaw leadership, for obvious reasons, tends to pad the number of Jews now living in Poland. Two calendars are published annually by the Warsaw leadership, one containing eighty pages and the other over two hundred. Both are printed in Polish. A message from the Chief Rabbi, Pinchas Menachem Joskowicz, appears on the last page of the calendars. The calendars also include a listing of the Jewish communities in Poland, with population statistics and some other details, but according to Mr. Lippman, the statistics are inflated. Indeed, my own perusal of the calendars revealed many errors. For instance, the 1989 calendar gives the blessing for water as "*Shehakol yihieh beseder,*" with, on the opposite side, an exact transliteration into Polish of this bizarre mistake.

As far as Katowice is concerned, however, Mr. Lippman declared that he was fully prepared to provide exact information. There are 122 Jews living in Katowice today, Mr. Lippman said. Only three Katowice

Jewish men are married to Jewish women. There is the Guttman family, whose son recently underwent circumcision in anticipation of becoming a bar mitzvah, a story that was picked up by the American press. The second Jewish family is headed by Shloimele Lefkowitz, whose son is a medical doctor somewhere in New York. Mr. Lippman's is the third Jewish family. The remaining men who attend synagogue services in Katowice do not have Jewish wives.

Services are held in the Katowice synagogue on Sabbaths and on holidays, with a minimum of twenty men in attendance and a few women. There is always a *kiddush* after prayers. The only person who can lead the services and read the Torah is Mr. Romankewitz, whose wife is *"nisht fun unsere"* ("not one of ours"). A daily kosher lunch, sponsored by the Joint Distribution Committee, is served in Katowice, attended by sixty Jews from the town and nearby areas. The state of disrepair of the Katowice cemetery is reaching crisis proportions, Mr. Lippman declared.

Referring to the calendar printed by the Warsaw leadership and amending it on the basis of his own knowledge, Mr. Lippman provided me with the following information about what is left of Jewish life in some of Poland's major cities.

Bielsko (Biala): 50 Jews. There is a community building, but no prayer services are held. Eighteen kosher lunches, sponsored by the Joint Distribution Committee, are served daily to Jews from the town and the neighboring areas.

Bytom: 40 Jews. Services are held on holidays, *yahrzeit* days, and *yizkor* days only.

Gliwice: 68 Jews. Services are held Saturdays and holidays, attended by about 35 men and fifteen women. The cemetery is well maintained.

Katowice: 122 Jews. Religious services are held on Sabbaths and on holidays. Kosher lunches are served five days a week for sixty people.

Krakow: 200 Jews. Services are held on Sabbaths and on holidays in the Remu Synagogue. Kosher lunches are served five days a week for fifty people. There is a *mikvah* in Krakow, the only one in Poland, located in Dr. Thons Temple (a reform temple before the war) on Ulica Miodowa 24, where services are occasionally held when there are many tourists visiting the city. The "Isaac Reb Yekeles" synagogue is now being remodeled by the Polish government. The cemetery is in good order.

Legnica: 60 Jews. Religious services are held on Saturdays and holidays. Kosher lunches are served five days a week for 22 people.

Lodz: 300 Jews. There are services on Saturdays and on holidays, and lunches five days a week for sixty people. Lodz is a well-organized Jewish community, probably the largest remaining in Poland.

Szczecin: 40 Jews. There are no religious services.

Warsaw: 200 Jews. There is only one synagogue in Warsaw where daily, Sabbath, and holiday services are held. Ten to fifteen Jews are paid by Rabbi Joskowicz's office to attend daily prayers. The Rabbi teaches a daily class in *Mishnayot* in the late after noon, between *mincha* and *maariv* services. On Shabbat, there are an additional forty to fifty Jews, usually guests and tourists, who attend services along with the ten to fifteen regulars. Lunches are served five days a week to sixty people and the *kashrut* of the kitchen is overseen by the rabbi. There is also an old-age home with about 22 residents. The cemeteries are kept in excellent order.

Wroclaw: 100 Jews. Sabbath and holiday services are held, and a daily lunch is served to forty people.

The total Jewish population of Poland, according to Mr. Lippman's estimate, is approximately 3,600 people. Of these, about 1,200 are members of their local community organizations.

However, Mr. Finkelstein of the Warsaw community claims that there are 10,000 Jews in Poland today, while others in his office say there are five to six thousand. Cardinal Dombrowsky, the right-hand man of Cardinal Glemp, recently disclosed to some visitors from the United States that there are only 1,900 Jews now living in Poland. On my first return trip to Poland in 1959, there were 30,000 Jews. In 1989, all agreed that there were about 15,000. After Passover, 1990, the figures declined from 10,000 to approximately 2,000 Jewish souls.

Mrs. Biener's answer to my question, *"Vos hert sich in Poilen?"* ("What's new in Poland") once again reverberated in my ear: *"Es halt shoin by Neilah,"* she had said; "it is the hour of the closing of the gate."

Chapter 43.
OSWIECIM, MY OSHPITZIN

Whenever I tell people that I grew up in Oswiecim, better known as Auschwitz, their eyes open in amazement and they are overcome with pity for me. "From Auschwitz, that accursed place?" they ask. It takes considerable explaining on my part to convince them that Oswiecim/Auschwitz, or Oshpitzin, as the Jews used to call it, was once a good and beautiful town.

It was in Oswiecim that I spent my youth. In those days, it was a town bursting with Jewish life and activities. I was six months old when my family moved to Oswiecim. This is where I grew up, studied at *cheder* and at *yeshivot*. This is where I became involved in the religious Zionist movement as a member of the Hashomer Hadati youth group. When I came to the United States in my mid-teens with my parents, we left behind one of my brothers, and some of my sisters, I left behind many dear friends, neighbors, and relatives. The Jews of Oswiecim comprised a close-knit community, almost like a large, extended family. Although, as in all developed Jewish communities, there were social, ideological, religious, class, and other differences among the Jews of Oswiecim, one common denominator bound us all together: we were all Jews.

There were many incidents in my youth to remind me of who I was and where my allegiance lay. I remember how, during recess at school, we Jews never went out into the playing field for fear of being attacked by Polish students. One cold, winter day, when the school yard was filled with snow, the bell rang for recess and we Jews, as usual, remained in our place. On that occasion, however, I suggested that we all go out together, and if we are attacked, that we fight back. We appeared outside on the "battlefield," and just as we expected, the Polish students began hurling snowballs at us. I picked up a handful of snow, ran over to one of our attackers, and pushed it into his face. Following my lead, my companions did the same. In short order, the bullies fled. It required only a few days of repeating this performance for the attacks to end. Our "enemies" never grew to love us, of course, but at least we had put some fear into their hearts.

Oswiecim, in southern Poland, is a small town in western Galicia, located about 35 miles from Krakow, 20 miles from Katowice, about 190 miles from Warsaw, and about 200 miles from Wroclaw or Breslau. The town is a central railroad point from all directions in Europe, close to the borders of Austria, Germany, Czechoslovakia, Russia, and Hungary. It is 220 miles from Prague, 200 miles from Vienna, and 330 miles from Berlin. This central location is what no doubt inspired Himmler to select Oswiecim as the ideal collecting point for the carrying out of the nefarious program to exterminate European Jewry.

Though situated near a mountainous area, Oswiecim itself is low and flat, with occasional marshy areas. Before the war, the town had a population of 12,000, of which 7,000 were Jews. The name by which the Jews called the town, "Oshpitzin," is a Polish corruption of the word "*Ushpizin*," or guests, in tribute to the well-known hospitality of its Jewish residents to travelers and wayfarers. The Poles often mispronounced Jewish words, sometimes inadvertently, sometimes deliberately. For a long time after the Bobover Rebbe made his grand visit to the town, for instance, the Poles continued to sing the Hebrew greeting song "*Kol Rina*" with a peculiar, comical pronunciation and accent.

Like Jews all over Galicia, Oswiecim's Jews earned their livelihood from business, trade, and peddling. In pre-war days, Oswiecim's Jews would travel daily by train with their merchandise to Katowice, Myslowice, and other town in upper Silesia, returning in the evening or on Friday to partake of a day that was wholly Sabbath. An old diary records how "There were many Jews from Oshpitzin who went to live and work in other cities. However, in their old age, they always returned to their hometown. The saying was, 'It is a good thing to live in a large city, but the best place for a Jew to die is Oshpitzin,' because the *tzaddikim* who were buried in Oshpitzin made the earth *admat kodesh*, holy ground."

While volumes have been written about Auschwitz, very little has been recorded about Oswiecim prior to its notorious transformation. The town, before the war, was a center of Jewish life, with pious Jews in beards and sidelocks, white stockings and *shtreimlach*, chassidim of Bobova, Belz, Sanz, and Radomsk with their own synagogues and *shtiblach*, their own *yeshivot* and *chadorim*. The Etz Chaim schools sponsored by the Bobover chassidim were especially popular in Oswiecim as they were throughout western Galicia. Chassidim would come to Oswiecim from all over Galicia to visit Reb Eluzerl, the son-in-law of the Sanzer Tzaddik, Rabbi Chaim Halberstam. In addition to the chassidim, there were, in Oswiecim, Jews of every persuasion-- General Zionists, Labor Zionists, Religious Zionists, Revisionists, Agudah members, Talmudic scholars, and secular Jews as well. The community leaders of Oswiecim included Alfred Haberfeld, Wolf Landau, Yaakov Wulkan, Naftali Bochner, Avraham Gross, Yitzchak Schnitzer, and Rudolf Haberfeld.

Many of the youth in Oswiecim lived, in those days before the war, with the hope that someday there would be a Jewish State in Eretz Israel. In anticipation of that day, many, myself included, were active in Zionist youth movements, and attended *hachsharot* in preparation for eventual *aliyah*. These young people were inspired in their Zionist ideology by their leaders, as well as by the education they received at home and in school.

When I returned to Oswiecim for the first time in 1959, I found only three Jews living there. Today, there is only one, and he, too, will most likely soon be leaving to join relatives in the United States. So much horror has passed over this town since that wonderful day in my youth when the Bobover Rebbe visited Oswiecim, and his chassidim, dressed in bright uniforms, came out on horseback in an honor guard to greet him. That Friday night, the entire community gathered in the 3,000-seat main synagogue to hear the Rebbe speak. It was a Shabbat that no one would ever forget.

The synagogue of Oswiecim was destroyed in the war. Soon the town's last Jew will be gone. All that remains in Oswiecim, besides the well-maintained cemetery supported by Jews in the United States and elsewhere, are the bones and ashes of the millions who were murdered in Auschwitz. Today, my Oshpitzin, the Oshpitzin of my childhood is no place for a Jew.

Chapter 44.
OSWIECIM'S JEWISH COMMUNITY

Historically, the question is often asked, Which came first, Poland or Oswiecim? In his 1938 volume published in Krakow, Dr. J. M. Potok points out that on the 1150 "Map of Adris" of Adrisi ben Abdulah (1100-1166), an Arab geographer who spent fifteen years creating, on a large silver tablet, a map based on his travels throughout Europe, Oswiecim is shown as a flourishing town even before Poland existed as a nation.

The beginnings of Jewish life in Oswiecim, as in the entire Poland, has long been a subject of historical speculation. The historian, Dr. Yitzchak Schipper, could not pinpoint an exact date for the arrival of Jews to Poland, but there is general agreement that Oswiecim existed as a town well before Poland was ruled by kings, and, according to some authorities, Jews were already thriving in Oswiecim from its earliest days.

One legend has it that Jews fleeing persecution in other parts of Europe arrived in Poland and declared, "*Po lin*" (in Hebrew, here we shall rest), and settled there. Another legend pointing to the presence of Jews in Poland as early as medieval times tells of a gathering in the ninth century of Polish leaders in the town of Kruszwica to choose a new king after the death of Prince Fofail. They decided that the first person to enter the town on a particular day would become the new ruler. This happened to be a Jew, Abraham Pruchownik, who became so alarmed at the prospect of becoming king, that he asked for three days to think the matter over. On the third day, he locked himself in his house, refusing to come out. The house was broken down, and Pruchownik, in desperation, successfully implored the local *pyast* (prince or landowner) of Kruszwica to become king in his stead.

A third legend describes how, in 893 CE, Jews escaping persecution in Germany sent a plea to the Polish Prince Laczek, requesting permission to settle on his lands. The Prince asked these Jews to describe the fundamentals of their religion, and, in the year 905, he granted them the right to settle in parts of what was to become Poland and to raise crops and animals there. Oswiecim was one of the cities in which the Jews were given permission to live.

It is generally agreed that Jews lived in Oswiecim and nearby Chrzanow for many centuries. The Jewish population of Oswiecim swelled after each Crusade, when persecution in Germany forced them to flee eastward to seek refuge. In 1470, the entire town was consumed by fire. Another fire in 1503 destroyed most of Oswiecim's houses as well as its palace, leaving only the foundation. The palace was said to have been made of wood, with a stone foundation.

To a large extent it can be said that the Jewish population of Oswiecim grew as a result of persecution elsewhere. Because of its central location, Jews fled to Oswiecim to escape the anti-Semitic decrees of Rindfleisch in the thirteenth century, and of Armleider in the fourteenth. Throughout the years of the Black Plague (1348-1352), Jews found refuge in Poland, and in Oswiecim in particular. The town, true to its name "Oshpitizin," always welcomed refugees. While Oswiecim had its share of pogroms, blood libels, and anti-Semitic violence, Jews were able to live and practice their religion in relative freedom. It is ironic that the place that had once served as a refuge to the persecuted became, in the end, the symbol of the greatest persecution in the history of the world.

In 1772, Poland was divided, with Austria taking over the entire area of Galicia, including Oswiecim. German, as well as Polish, became the primary languages of the townspeople, and even after the First World War, when Poland gained its independence and Polish became the country's official language, German, or a mixture of Polish and German, could still be heard in Oswiecim. During the Austrian occupation, an army camp was built outside the town limits, consisting of sixteen one-story brick barracks, which the locals called the "*Baraken*.." These were situated on the swampy lands not far from the

Sola River, a branch of the Vistula. In 1851, the population of Oswiecim was 2,500. By 1939, there were over 12,000 people living in the town.

Until the outbreak of the Second World War, Jews lived in Poland--and in Oswiecim--for centuries, contributing enormously to the cultural, religious, artistic, economic, and scholarly life of the country. In his responsa, the Rema writes: "I prefer to have a piece of dry bread and live in peace in this country (Poland) where hatred is not so great as in German lands." Such expressions as "Without Poland there is no blessing" testify to the affection that Jews had for their country, an affection that was, in the end, bitterly betrayed.

Chapter 45.
OSWIECIM AND THE
"COUNCIL OF FOUR LANDS"

Between 1580 and 1764, Poland's large Jewish population enjoyed a considerable degree of autonomy through the "Council of Four Lands," or the *Vaad Arba Arazot*. The *Vaad*'s activities encompassed charitable, judicial, and administrative functions, and, in fact, constituted a form of self-government that included a special rabbinical court guided by *halachic* and Talmudic legislation, which decided on cases involving civil law. Whenever a *halachic* problem arose that could not be solved by local rabbis, the great rabbinic authorities of the *Vaad* would be summoned to determine the outcome. Their decisions were final and accepted by all. Any problem between communities, or between a community and an individual in which one or another would not accept the verdict would be brought before the high court of appeals of the *Vaad*. Most of these rabbinic court sessions were held during the *yarid* (fairs), which took place several times a year in the cities of Jaroslaw or Lublin.

The records of the *Vaad* contain many references to cases involving litigants from Oswiecim, among them an exchange of letters between the community and the church. While many of the records have been lost, what remains, including letters, notes, some minutes, listings of names as well as of the Council's rulings, were collected by Professor Israel Halpern of the Hebrew University, and published in 1949 in his *Pinkas Vaad Arba Arazot*.

The Council of Four Lands was well respected by religious and secular Jews. The Baal Tosafot Yom Tov, Rabbi Yom Tov Lippman Heller, mentions the *Vaad* of 1635 in his book, *Megillat Evah*. Nathan Hanover describes the role and activities of the *Vaad* in this manner: "The representatives--*Parnesim*--of the four lands had sessions twice a year, at the fair in Lublin between Purim and Passover, and at the fair in Jaroslaw, Galicia, in the month of Av or Elul. The representatives resembled the *Sanhedrin* in the session chamber of the Temple of Jerusalem, *Lishkat Hagazit*. They had jurisdiction over all the Jews of the Kingdom of Poland and were empowered to issue injunctions and binding decisions--*takanot*--and to impose penalties at their discretion. Every difficult case was submitted for trial. To make the task easier, judges from each land (called 'Land Judges') were selected by the representatives of the Four Lands committee ('*Dayanei Medinah* ') to try civil suits, while criminal cases, disputes over priority of possessions--*chazaka*--and other difficult cases were tried in full session by the representatives themselves."

A community that wished to join the *Vaad* was required to make a formal application, which would be considered at one of the Council's regular sessions. In Professor Halpern's *Pinkas*, there is a record of a response to one such request, which was usually given in Hebrew or Yiddish: "We have this day granted the petition of the elders of Tiktin (Tykocin) recorded on page...for representation in the Council of Four Lands. We have acceded to their request that they be allowed to have a representative from this time forward in the manner set forth on page...and again on the page for today...These are the words of the Council of Four Lands, this day, Wednesday, 4 Sivan, at Lublin." What follows, then, are the signatures of the 21 members of the *Vaad*.

Oswiecim's best-known representative to the *Vaad* was its *Rav*, Rabbi Yitzchak Landau. In the *Pinkas* (minutes) of the *Vaad*, Rabbi Landau is cited as a "*Ne'eman*"--a trustee ("*Ne'eman b'Yisrael d'Arba Arazot*."). Rabbi Landau was born in Fitz in 1713, and came from Olkusz to serve as the rabbi of Oswiecim, where he died at the age of seventy, on the second of Iyar, 1783.

The reappearance of a blood libel in Oswiecim is mentioned three times in the *Pinkas*, and though not too many details are provided about the complexities of this case, it is clear that what was involved was the classical accusation that Jews murdered a Christian child to use his blood in Passover *matzot*. In order to prove their innocence, Oswiecim Jews were obliged to appear before the *Seim*, the Polish government.

Blood libels, however, continued to be a source of great concern in Oswiecim even in relatively modern times, well after the final sessions of the Council of Four Lands. In a newspaper report in the bi-weekly, *Machzikei Hadat*, over a hundred years ago, an Oswiecim reporter writes: "One Friday morning, *Erev Shabbat Hagadol*, one of our brothers of the Oshpitzin community returned from a nearby village where he had purchased merchandise for resale. Among his purchases he carried a basket covered with a towel in which a lamb lay crying for its mother. As he walked in the street, a Christian woman passed and heard the crying and believed it to be a Christian child soon to be killed by the Jews for his blood, to be used for Passover *matzot*. She alerted the police who entered the Jewish home, and searched it together with the Christian woman. This was the home of an honorable Jew from Oshpitzin named Rav Mordechai Schnitzer. When he returned from the *Maariv* service he was frightened to see the house surrounded by police and hundreds of Christian onlookers. They ordered him to show the baby, and when he denied this, he was taken from room to room along with the Christian woman. Suddenly they heard crying and the woman said, 'That's the Christian child he was carrying when he went by in the street.' The police removed the towel and discovered the lamb. Embarrassed, they left the house. The following day the newspaper contained an item about a Jew who was ready to slaughter a Christian child for his blood and only police intervention saved him."

Chapter 46.
CHASSIDIC MASTERS OF OSWIECIM

The chassidism of the Baal Shem Tov, at first maligned by Torah scholars, including his own brother-in-law, Rabbi Gershon Kitover, soon won over the hearts of thousands of Jews, and spread quickly from its origins in Podolia, to Lithuania and Poland, and throughout Galicia. In time, Oswiecim became an important center of chassidism.

There is a story told about two chassidic leaders, Reb Elimelech of Lizensk and his brother, Reb Zeesha of Hanipoli, who wandered from town to town. Upon reaching Oswiecim, Reb Zeesha declared to his brother, "This is the last stop." During the Holocaust, some chassidim interpreted these words as a dire prophecy of what, in the future, awaited the Jewish people in Oswiecim/ Auschwitz.

The two brothers remained in Oswiecim for many days, preaching and teaching chassidism. At first, some of the townspeople objected to the new philosophy, but in a short time, it became extremely popular, and many small *shtiblach* and houses of prayer were opened.

Reb Berish Frumer is generally regarded as the first *tzaddik* of Oswiecim. Born in Chrzanow, only ten miles from Oswiecim, his revered teacher was Reb Shlomo Bochner, a student of the great Reb Shmelke of Nikelsburg. Originally a businessman, Reb Shlomo Bochner, who died in 1828, grew to be respected as one of the great *gaonim* and *tzaddikim* of his generation. Reb Berish Frumer's other illustrious teacher was the Chozeh of Lublin, Rabbi Yaakov Yitzchak Horowitz. As a young man, Reb Berish served as a *melamed*, a teacher of young children, but went on to became a scholar of renown. He was especially popular in Oswiecim, where hundreds came to him for advice and he was regarded as a *"Baal Mofess."* Reb Berish authored several volumes, including *Divrei Tzaddikim*, which was published by his students after his death in 1838.

Rabbi Shlomo Halberstam was the second great chassidic master of Oswiecim. The son of Rabbi Meir Nosson Halberstam, and the grandson of the Sanzer Tzaddik, Rabbi Chaim Halberstam, author of *Divrei Chaim*, Reb Shlomo was a great Torah scholar who, like his distinguished forebears, taught that chassidism does not consist solely of visits to and admiration of the Rebbe, but also of a deep knowledge of Torah, *halacha,* and Talmud. He lived modestly, and was known for his acts of charity toward the many Jews who flocked to him in Oswiecim and toward the students who were drawn to his yeshiva.

From Oswiecim, Rabbi Shlomo Halberstam went on to Wisznice, near Krakow, where he remained for thirteen years. However, because of a heart ailment, he was advised by his doctors to settle in the mountainous area of Bobowa. There he established the Bobover dynasty with a thriving yeshiva. Thousands of chassidim would gather in Bobowa, particularly during the holidays. After his death in 1905, he was succeeded by his son, Rabbi Benzion Halberstam, the father of the present Bobover Rebbe, Rabbi Shlomo Halberstam. Although he had left Oswiecim, the town's Jews remembered their Rebbe with profound respect and admiration.

During the First World War, Reb Shloimele, the Tzaddik of Sassov, settled in Oswiecim and became the center of its chassidic life. As the grandson of Reb Sholom of Belz, Reb Shloimele was greatly inspired by the Belzer style of chassidism. Most of his followers were Torah scholars and learned man, and thousands of chassidim flocked to him from near and far. Immediately after the war, he returned to his hometown of Lemberg, where he died in 1918, but the Jews of Oswiecim remembered him as one of their own great chassidic masters.

Rabbi Elazar Halevi Rosenfeld, known affectionately as Reb Eluzerl Oshpitzner, was born in 1880, the son of Reb Yehoshua Rosenfeld, the Rabbi of Kaminker and a student of Reb Naftali Ropshitzer. Reb Eluzerl was married at age seventeen to the daughter of Rabbi Chaim Halberstam, the Sanzer Tzaddik, but because his father-in-law had died, he lived on *"kest"* at the home of his brother-in-law, Rabbi Shlomo Halberstam of Wisznice, studying Torah day and night. His first position was in Bochnia, and from there he moved on to

Oswiecim, where he served for many years as the town's chassidic master. He sat in his *bet medrash* studying Torah, receiving visitors, particularly the Sanzer and Bobover chassidim who supported him, and most of his income he gave to charity.

As a young boy growing up in Oswiecim, I remember Reb Eluzerl's fervent *davening*. Often, on a Friday night, I came and sat at his *tisch*, and, along with hundreds of chassidim, listened to the words he spoke and the *zemirot*. he sang. His *bet medrash* was on Ulica Berka Yoselowicza, where most of the synagogues and *yeshivot* were located. This *bet medrash*, which was next to the big synagogue and the *mikvah*, had a wall that separated the rabbi's dwelling and *shtibel* from a convent. The chassidim did not dare to touch this wall or come close to it. Before the Second World War, Reb Eluzerl settled in Israel, first in Zefat and later in the Mea Shearim section of Jerusalem, and despite the danger in those days, he did not hesitate to visit the Western Wall. In Jerusalem, he lived in great poverty, and was urged by his family to return to Oswiecim to be cured of an illness that afflicted him.

In 1939, Reb Eluzerl returned to Oswiecim, where he was able to remain until 1941, when the Nazis cut off his beard and sidelocks, as they did to so many other Jews. While most of the Jews who were driven out of Oswiecim went to Sosnowiec, Reb Eluzerl decided to go on to Chrzanow, where he died on the twentieth of Av, 1942, and, unlike most of Galicia's Jews, had the privilege of a proper burial.

One day in Chrzanow, according to an eyewitness account, the aged Reb Eluzerl Oshpitzner, who never read the newspapers or listened to the radio, was told that the Germans were celebrating Hitler's birthday by killing and attacking Jews. Reb Eluzerl recalled then. that fifty years earlier, he and some other students were sitting in the *bet medrash* of his brother-in-law, the Shiniver Tzaddik, Rabbi Yechezkel Halberstam, when suddenly Rabbi Halberstam cried out, "*Zogt Tehilim*--recite Psalms--for on this day, at this hour, an extraordinarily evil person is being born, more wicked than Haman, and we must pray to God that he is destroyed before he reaches maturity."

Indeed, Oswiecim was a town of many wonders. Chaim Wolnerman, one of the editors of *Sefer Oshpitzin*, published in 1977 in Jerusalem by Irgun Yotzei Oswiecim, describes one mysterious incident from his childhood. It happened in the winter of 1926, in Shenker's Shtibel, named for one of the wealthiest and most generous Jews of Oswiecim. Young Chaim was sitting with some boys, awaiting a lesson by Rabbi Asher Zelig Landau, when the group noticed, "in the corner, behind the burning stove, a Jew sitting at the table displaying some *seforim*. He was a short, skinny man, dressed in a long *kaopte*, a round, low hat on his head. He was selling his books....It was customary in those days to see a Jew selling *seforim* in *shul*."

"We hardly paid attention to this 'bookseller,'" Chaim Wolnerman goes on to say in his account. "When our *rosh yeshiva* entered, we rose in respect for our teacher. Our *rebbe* walked over to the table to see the *seforim* on display. Suddenly, our teacher bent over, fell on this old bookseller, embracing and kissing him.

"Needless to say, we were surprised to witness such a scene. However, to our *rosh yeshiva*, Reb Asher Zelig Landau, this man was not a stranger. This *mocher seforim* was known all over Poland. Our rebbe noticed our surprise and said, 'This *mocher seforim* is the great *gaon* and *tzaddik*, Rabbi Yisrael Meir HaKohen--the Chofetz Chaim from Radin.'"

In the Oswiecim of my youth, my family and I attended daily and Shabbat services in the synagogue of Reb Yankele Zukerberg, the Pomarner Rebbe, a descendant of the Komarno and Sassover Rebbes. He was a true student of Torah, and he was blessed with a beautiful voice that attracted many followers to him, to listen to his singing and to seek his advice. I became a bar mitzvah in his *bet medrash*, and prayed in his synagogue until my family and I emigrated to the United States. Just before the war, he moved to Komarno where he became the *Admor* of Sassov. For many years I have tried to discover what happened to my Rebbe, Reb Yankel Zukerberg, but with no success.

Chapter 47.
THE RABBIS OF OSWIECIM

In addition to such outstanding chassidic masters as Reb Berish Frumer, author of *Divrei Tzaddikim*, and Rabbi Shlomo Halberstam, the first Bobover Rebbe, Oswiecim was distinguished by a series of remarkable rabbis. Rabbi Yitzchak Landau, the town's representative to the Council of Four Lands, and the father-in-law of Rabbi Benjamin Wolff, author of *Shaarei Torah*, can rightfully be cited as Oswiecim's first "official" rabbi. He was followed by Rabbi Moshe Yaacov Sharf (1823-1908), a student of the Sanzer Tzaddik as well as of Rabbi Tzvi Hirsch Heller of Ungvar, author of *Tiv Gittin*.. Rabbi Sharf served as Oswiecim's rabbi for fifty years. His *Darkei Yosher* on the Talmud and the Bible was highly regarded by the scholars of his day.

As in many Jewish communities, there were differences of opinion in Oswiecim as to what qualities were desired in the town's leading rabbi. When a Talmudic scholar rose to prominence he was expected by the community to be knowledgeable in secular studies as well as in Jewish learning. However, the chassidim of the town always preferred a *tzaddik* or an *admor* , and when a more broadly educated rabbi gained acceptance, they would flock more closely around their Rebbe. Rabbi Dr. Ephraim Israel Blecher, who was born in 1813 in Glucksdorf, Moravia, was one such spiritual leader who began his career as a professor of Semitic languages at the University of Lemberg. He became the rabbi of Oswiecim in 1856, and later moved on to Wadowice, from where he served as rabbi of the entire area. He was the author of a work on Hebrew grammar, *Marpe Lashon Arami*, as well as of an 1862 German translation of the Book of Ruth, a Hebrew-German-Hungarian dictionary, and a geography of Palestine. He died in Budapest, Hungary in 1881.

Rabbi Abele Shnur served as Oswiecim's rabbi for nineteen years, from 1881 to 1900, when he moved on to become the spiritual leader of Tarnow, a much larger city. Widely respected for his Torah and his secular learning, as well as for his deeds of charity and community involvement, Rabbi Shnur was often compared to Rabbi Jonathan Eibeschitz of Prague. Fluent in German and French in addition to his native Polish, Hebrew, and Yiddish, Rabbi Shnur was frequently invited to lecture in Jewish communities in western Europe.

Rabbi Shnur traveled throughout Germany to collect money for the destitute refugees of the Kishinev pogrom. Many of these unfortunate souls had fled to western Galicia, arriving in Oswiecim with the hope of traveling on to Germany and the United States, but because of a lack of funds were unable to continue their journey. Rabbi Shnur made their cause his own, and he did not rest until each one of these refugees was on his way to a free country where he might begin life anew.

When the families of 180 Jews who were accused of smuggling merchandise and imprisoned in Wadowice petitioned Rabbi Shnur for help, he turned immediately to a friend in Vienna who arranged for a meeting between the rabbi and Kaiser Franz Josef of Austria. After spending eight days in Vienna, Rabbi Shnur returned home bearing an order from the emperor for the release of the Jews at once, with no trial. Rabbi Shnur never spoke of this incident until years later, when, at a conference of rabbis in Krakow, a chassidic leader turned to him, and citing Rabbi Shnur as one who, although not a chassid himself, had done more than most *tzaddikim*, he pleaded with Rabbi Shnur to reveal, at last, what had transpired between him and the emperor.

"I threatened the Kaiser," Rabbi Shnur said.

All eyes turned to the rabbi as he continued. "When I presented the case before the Kaiser and pleaded with him to free the Jews, he asked me if, as a rabbi, I did not believe that these men deserved their punishment. I replied that I believed they had suffered enough. They had been imprisoned for over two weeks, they had been separated from their wives and children, all their merchandise had been confiscated, and heavy penalties had been levied against them. The Kaiser then declared that he preferred not to involve himself in local affairs. To that I responded that since the Jews of Oswiecim are so poor and the king is so wealthy and good-hearted, surely he would not mind if the suffering wives and children of these 180 prisoners moved into his palace until their husbands and fathers could be released and resume providing for them.

"At that," Rabbi Shnur continued, "the Kaiser laughed, thought a minute, and ordered me to go to the Minister of Justice who, the next day, handed me a sealed order to the directors of the Wadowice prison to release the Jews."

Another Oswiecim rabbi who was also knowledgeable in secular studies was Rabbi Dr. Leibish Mintz who was a graduate of the Yeshiva Chatam Sofer after having studied earlier in Hungary. His departure from Oswiecim to the prestigious position of rabbi of Kepina, near Poznan, the city where the Malbim had served for meany years, was precipitated by an event that scandalized the town's Jewish community. Rabbi Mintz had angered certain devout members of the community because of his strenuous objection to the tradition of performing a *chupah* in a cemetery as protection against a plague that was afflicting Oswiecim during his term there, and he was supported in his objection by the local police. The following Rosh Hashanah, when Rabbi Mintz rose to the *bima* for the shofar blowing, one of the congregants, Yisrael Tobias, pushed him aside and declared, "The holy sounds of the shofar were not made for students of Latin! If we need you to intercede in our behalf with the *goyim*, we'll send for you. But now we need someone to intercede for us with the Almighty, and you are not that person."

When Rabbi Mintz admonished him, Tobias raised his hand and slapped the rabbi across the face in front of the entire congregation. The worshippers were furious, and the police were called in. The rabbi performed his duties through the Succot holiday, and then left Oswiecim, unable to accept the humiliation he had endured. He died in 1920 after authoring several important books.

Another notable rabbi in Oswiecim was Rabbi Chaim Tzvi Kuperman, who served the community for forty years as judge and spiritual leader. He was a disciple of Rabbi Berish Frumer, and was buried beside his teacher in the cemetery of Oswiecim.

Rabbi Yehoshua Pinchas Bombach was renowned as a scholar for his book of reponsa, *Ohel Yehoshua*.. His yeshiva in Oswiecim attracted many students and scholars. Upon his death in 1920, his position was passed on to his son, Rabbi Eliyahu Bombach. With most of Oswiecim's Jews, Rabbi Eliyahu Bombach was transported by the Nazis first to Sosnowiec, and from there back to Auschwitz. According to an eyewitness account, he perished on Lag BaOmer, 1943. I knew Rabbi Bombach and his family when I was a boy. His son, Isaac, was my friend. Isaac Bombach never married, and he never returned from the forced labor camp to which he had been sent.

Chapter 48.
OSWIECIM BEFORE THE SECOND
WORLD WAR

Jewish life in Oswiecim proceeded in a fairly normal fashion in the years before World War II. Of course, everyone worried about the expansion and build-up of the German military and about the annexation of territory by Hitler. It was not until *Kristallnacht*, 1938, however, that real fear began to penetrate the hearts of Polish Jewry, and some of Oswiecim's Jews started planning for the eventuality that war might break out.

I recall a visit by a Polish army officer to our school in Oswiecim. He told us about the deep hatred that the Germans bore for the Polish people, and especially for those of Jewish descent. A Jew was never mentioned, he informed us, without a pejorative epithet, *verfluchter Jude* or *Polisher Schwein* being among the most common.

Yet despite the heightened antagonism between the Poles and the Germans, the Jews of Oswiecim carried on with their day to day affairs, engaging in *husiren* (peddling), traveling to such towns close to Germany as Katowice or Myslowice, and even to Bytom on the Polish-German border. These daily journeys were always accompanied by a great deal of bustle in the *Rynek*, which fascinated and excited me as a child, as I watched people fight for places in droshkies and other conveyances that would carry them from the main marketplace to the railway station. The trains were always filled to capacity. Many of Oswiecim's Jewish men worked very hard, traveling every day, leaving home before dawn, and returning late at night or at the week's end for Shabbat..

I remember one night hearing the cries of a Jewish peddler. He was being accosted by a gentile, who thought that the bag the peddler was carrying was filled with money. When the gentile grabbed the bag and tore it open, he found that it contained only apples that the peddler was bringing home to his family. So furious was the gentile at this discovery, that he continued to pummel the Jew until the police we had called arrived on the scene.

Life was not easy for the Jews of Oswiecim, but somehow we managed. When the Sabbath came, everything took on a new and fresh appearance. Families were together for a full twenty-four hours. My father would take me and my brother by the hand, and together we would walk to *shul*. My mother and sisters would follow some time later. Everyone in the street seemed a little taller and more erect, free, during this one day of rest from the week's travail. The father would test the children on what they had learned during the previous week--*Chumash, Rashi, Gemara*--and they had better be well prepared or they would have an earache for the entire week following. Pulling a child's ear was the standard punishment for failing to do well in one's studies.

When I was three years old, my brother and I were taken to *cheder* for the first time. The *melamed* was the famous Reb Eliezer Zlotorow, a tall Jew with a long beard who was known as "Lazar Fonie" because he came from upper Poland. As I would enter the *cheder*, he would take hold of my little ear, pull it lightly, and say, "This is the pull of love." I understood what he meant when I did well in my reading, but when I would make a mistake, he would grab the same ear, and this time it was not the pull of love. I would cry, and he would give me a *zikerl*, a candy, and I was all better. I dared not make mistakes any more.

After one year in *cheder*, I began to study Leviticus, *Vayikrah*. I was four years old, and Reb Lazar tried to explain to me about sacrifices. The next year, in order to start *Chumash* in earnest, my father was supposed to have reported to the *melamed* that he had tested me on everything that had been covered previously. I remember coming into the *cheder* that Sunday morning in August when I was five and standing in front of Reb Lazar with my brother, only one year older, at my side. "*Yingele*," Reb Lazar asked, holding on to my ear, "*der tate hot dich fahertt?*" ("Little boy, did your father test you?") As it happened, my father had been away for the Sabbath, visiting his Rebbe in another town. I turned to my brother, who nodded, and I nodded in turn to Reb Lazar Fonie. I was moved to the table of the older students, and from that day on I began to learn *Chumash Ki-Tetze*. I didn't tell a lie, I said to myself. I only nodded.

Besides Reb Lazar Fonie, other *melamdim* in Oswiecim at that time included Reb Sholom Kahana, Reb Aharon Korngold, Reb Avraham Wilchford, and the Lodzer Melamed. Soon enough, I was studying *Gemara* and *Tosafot*, and upon the advice of the Bobover Rebbe, Rabbi Benzion Halberstam, at whose court I had spent the Succot holiday, I was sent to another town to study at a Bobover yeshiva.

In addition to my studies, I became involved, in Oswiecim, with the Hashomer Hadati, the Religious Zionist youth organization of the Mizrachi. We dreamed of the day that we could go to Palestine and establish our own Jewish state there. One of our favorite songs was "*Shtei Gidot LaYarden,*" ("There Are Two Sides to the Jordan"), which we sang with gusto even though it was a Revisionist hymn. Our group was ready to take on the Polish bullies at any time. I remember how my brother and I were attacked one night on our way home from *cheder* by a boy named Bubetz. We scratched his shaved head and gave him a good thrashing but when we thought we had finished him off, he suddenly surprised us by picking up a sharp stone and cutting into my brother's cheek, leaving a two-inch scar which would still be visible today if not for his beard and sidelocks that cover it.

Of course, chassidim constituted only one element of Oswiecim's Jewish community. There were religious Jews who were not chassidim, and there were modern, secular Jews as well. Despite the differences that existed, however, Oswiecim's Jewish community was a relatively cohesive and united one, and as Hitler's dark shadow loomed ever more menacingly over the town, its Jews, out of their sense of the common danger and the common fate that awaited them, drew closer and closer together for comfort and support.

Chapter 49.
OSWIECIM AT THE OUTBREAK OF THE WAR

Jewish peddlers from Oswiecim who traveled to upper Silesia, to Katowice, Myslowice, or even Bytom on the Polish-German border, began returning with grim tales about what was happening in Germany. Their reports, far more accurate than the censored newspaper accounts, were particularly alarming in the light of the Nazis' expansionist ambitions, for the fate of German Jewry might soon engulf the Jews of Poland as well.

On October 1, 1933, the Germans issued a boycott against Jewish merchants, prohibiting the patronizing of Jewish-owned establishments or the buying of manufactured goods from Jewish concerns. This boycott was enforced by the Nazis with their usual zeal and efficiency. Two years later, on September 1, 1935, the Nuremberg anti-Jewish laws were passed, banning mixed marriages between Jews and non-Jews and revoking German citizenship from all Jews. As a consequence of these laws, all Polish-born Jews living in Germany were sent back to Poland.

The Commander-in-Chief of the Polish Army, Marshall Ridz-Szmigly, responding to the aggressive movements of Germany that affected not only Jews but Poland, too, issued a strong statement: ''We shall not give in to the Germans. Not even one button shall we yield.'' In the meantime, conditions throughout Germany, Poland, and the entire Europe grew increasingly worse. From Paris came the report that a young Jew, Herschel Greenspan, had assassinated a high German official, Ernst von Rath.

On October 12, 1938, Hitler gave Hermann Goering the authority to oversee the "Final Solution" for the Jewish people. At first, the plan was to drive the Jews out of Germany and confiscate their property, which would be transferred to the Hermann Goering Foundation. Less than a month later, on November 9, 1938, the infamous *Kristallnacht* took place, in which hundreds of synagogues in Germany were destroyed, and Jewish property was attacked, pillaged, and robbed. Only a few months after this event, on January 8, 1939, Jewish emigration from Germany was given new urgency with the appointment of Dr. H. Schacht, president of the German National Bank, to speed up the process. Then, on the twenty-fourth of the month, full charge of the "Jewish problem" was put into the hands of Reinhardt Heydrich.

The Jews of Oswiecim watched these developments across the border with profound concern. While some Jews, such as Willy Kuperman who completed the construction of a beautiful new villa for himself just before the war broke out, believed that events in Germany would have no serious effect on Poland, others began to take measures to escape what they perceived to be a great danger. Plans were made to leave Oswiecim in a direction as far away as possible from Germany on the west. Czechoslovakia to the south was, of course, already under Nazi domination. Some Oswiecim Jews went to Lublin, on the way to Lithuania at the northern border. Others sought to go east, to Russia.

On August 30, 1939, Hitler delivered his famous speech in the Reichstag, and the outbreak of war seemed only a matter of time. Two days later, on September 1, 1939, Germany invaded Poland. Nazi planes bombed Oswiecim on the very first day of the war, destroying two houses on Ulica Kosczelna, near the school and church. Fortunately, the Jews who had lived in those homes had left the town just a day earlier. During that first bombardment of Oswiecim, a German fighter plane was shot down and its pilot parachuted to safety. His life was saved by a Jew.

According to one eyewitness, on the following day, which was a Saturday, September 2, 1939, the roads were crowded with Jews, many in chassidic garb, babies on their backs and their entire families following on foot or in hired wagons. These refugees hoped to reach Krakow in advance of the German army, and from there make their way to Tarnow, then Przemysl, Lvov, and onward as close as possible to the Russian border. Unfortunately, they were stopped by German soldiers, who forced them to turn back to Oswiecim. On September 3, 1939, a German engineering corps unit entered the town to restore the bridge that had been destroyed by the Polish army in order to prevent German entry into the town. On that day, a Sunday, the Nazis ordered the Jews of Oswiecim to gather in the *Rynek*. There in the town square, eight people were murdered.

The *Rynek*, which had once been the heart of so much life, had now become the center of death. This *Rynek* in Oswiecim consisted of about two or three acres of land, surrounded by Jagelonska, Koleyowa, Plebanska, and Zatorska Streets, as well as by Berka Yoselowicza, the Jewish street. Ninety percent of the buildings around the *Rynek* belonged to and were occupied by Jews. All of the shops in the houses, with the exception of the butcher shop and the grocery, were owned by Jews. After the Nazis took over Poland, this *Rynek* became the scene of forced deportations, beatings, murders, and a host of cruelties and atrocities that continued until not a single Jew remained in Oswiecim.

Chapter 50.
OSWIECIM DURING THE FIRST MONTH OF
THE WAR

Before candle lighting, on Friday, September 1, 1939, the day Germany invaded Poland, two Oswiecim Jews, the wealthy businessman Leo "Eliezer" Shenker and a companion, heard a plane crash into a field near Shenker's villa. From their flattened position to escape the bombing, they watched in amazement as a man attached to what seemed like a giant umbrella floated to the ground and struggled to disentangle himself from the ropes that harnessed him to his strange contraption. The man was wounded and bleeding, and the two Jews ran to his aid and carried him into a nearby house.

He was a German pilot whose plane had been shot down by Polish anti-aircraft guns. His co-pilot had been killed in the attack. The surviving pilot's leg and several teeth were broken. The Jews tended the wounded man and did not inform Polish authorities of his presence. When the Germans entered Oswiecim on the third of September, the Jews led them to the wounded man, who, it turned out, was an important Nazi officer.

While the Nazis could not really understand why the Jews had gone to so much trouble to save a German life, they were nevertheless grateful. Leo Shenker, a leader, of the Oswiecim Jewish community, became friendly with the wounded Nazi officer, and as a result of this connection was in a position to gain many favors for the Jews. Accordingly, the other leaders of the Jewish community--Avraham

Gross, Avraham Yachtzel the *gabbai*, Aharon Silbiger, Michael Sander, Yosef Manheimer, and Heshko Silbiger--elected Israel Shenker to the position of *rosh hakahal* of the community, and promised him their full cooperation.

The Jews who had been returned by the Nazis to Oswiecim after attempting to escape eastward reported that the Germans were burning synagogues in Trzebinia and in other towns and that 32 Jews had been murdered in a forest near Wieliczka. Leo Shenker approached von Grief, the German commander of Oswiecim, to inquire about these reports. Von Grief informed Shenker that the execution of the Jews was in reprisal against Polish citizens who had killed Germans living in Poland.

Reports of Nazi atrocities continued to come in during the entire period of the High Holy Days. As the Jews of Oswiecim gathered in their synagogue to pray by candlelight, for there was no longer any electricity, they could hear the Nazis goosestepping outside. Leo Shenker ordered that two large boxes be constructed in which to hide the Torahs and the other holy articles and silver utensils.

In the meantime, the German soldiers went wild. They lined up chassidic Jews and forced the men to cut off their beards and sidelocks. Oswiecim Jews wept to see the shorn face of Reb Eluzerl, the son-in-law of the Reb Chaim Halberstam, the Sanzer Tzaddik. Even so, Reb Eluzerl managed to pray with his chassidim on Rosh Hashana and Yom Kippur in his *shtibel*, and the rabbi and cantor conducted services in the main synagogue. The *mikvah* was in full operation throughout the holidays. It was Leo Shenker, thanks to his friendship with the wounded German officer, who had arranged for a temporary reprieve from the forced labor to which the Nazis had assigned the Jews so that the holidays could be observed.

When the Nazis decreed that only Aryans could operate a business, Shenker paid Poles to permit their names to be listed as the owners of establishments that continued to be run by Jews. Shenker also intervened to save twelve priests who were condemned to be shot because some old guns had been found in their church on Ulica Jagelonska. The Germans had ordered that no citizen could possess arms or ammunition on penalty of death, and all weapons had been confiscated. Shenker went to the German commander and explained that the weapons that had been found in the church were old, broken, discarded, and forgotten. Naturally, the Nazi commander was astonished that a Jew should plead to save the lives of a group of Christians. Nevertheless, the matter was investigated, and upon inspection, Shenker was proved right and the priests were released.

On September 20, 1939, the main synagogue of Oswiecim was set on fire by the Nazis. The Germans surrounded the building and would not allow anyone to approach to save the Torah scrolls or the sacred objects. The entire structure and forty scrolls were demolished on that day, and it seemed to the Jews of Oswiecim that their Jewish life had been extinguished as it had been in the time of the destruction by the Romans of the Second Temple.

Only the *gabbai*, Avraham Yachtzel, continued to hope, and he sought to raise the spirits of his people. "We shall rebuild our synagogue," he cried. "The new one will be even more beautiful. And if we cannot do it, our children will. And if we cannot build it here in Oswiecim, we shall build it in our holy city of Jerusalem."

These events that transpired in Oswiecim during the first month of the war were reported to me by one of the town's few Jewish survivors. Over the ensuing months, the entire population of what had been a flourishing center of Jewish life disappeared, but not before a bizarre figure appeared on the scene--Israel Monik Marion, a Jew bearing a letter from Heinrich Himmler. The letter read: "Israel Monik Marion appears before you on my personal introduction. All German officers are to obey his orders as if I had given them."

Left: The Auschwitz ovens;
Rabbi Moshe Weiss, reciting
prayer

Above: Inside the Auschwitz camp

Below: Inmates slept in these cubicles

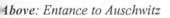

Above: Entance to Auschwitz

Right: Death Wall
in Auschwitz

Left: The building of the
new convent in Auschwitz,
not completed and not
occupied

Right: The present
convent, front view

Chapter 51.
ISRAEL MONIK MARION AND THE GERER REBBE'S BLESSING

"Your destroyers and despoilers will come from you," the prophet Isaiah teaches. Such an individual was the Jew, Israel Monik Marion, who was well known for his unsavory and treacherous activities not only in Oswiecim, but also in Sosnowiec, Katowice, and the surrounding areas, and even in Berlin.

On two separate occasions, Leo Shenker, the leader of the Oswiecim Jewish community, had been warned about Marion. As a member of a delegation of Polish Jews that met in Berlin with Rabbi Leo Baeck, chairman of the United Congregations of Berlin and chief rabbi of that city, Shenker had been advised by Rabbi Baeck himself to be on his guard with respect to Monik Marion of Sosnowiec. Marion, Rabbi Baeck told Shenker, had an office in the Gestapo headquarters in Sosnowiec and was closely connected to Himmler, whose letter of introduction he carried with him wherever he went.

Major von Grief, the Nazi administrator of Oswiecim, was the second person who cautioned Shenker about Marion. Von Grief, on orders from Berlin, issued decrees that all Oswiecim Jews wear yellow identifying badges, that all Jewish gold and businesses be confiscated, that Jewish beards be cut, and that Jews be assigned to perform menial, humiliating labor. Yet before his departure with his unit which was being transferred from Oswiecim, at the villa of Dr. Druks, von Grief remembered Shenker's connection to the rescued pilot, and, in gratitude, he gave the Jewish leader a letter designed to protect him. In addition, von Grief took Shenker aside and warned him to beware of Monik Marion.

This second warning motivated Shenker to seek out information about Marion. His inquiries, at first, yielded no results, but eventually he learned from a Katowice Jew who had been transferred to Oswiecim that Marion had been appointed *Gruppen Fuehrer* of the young Jews who had been sent to Sosnowiec to do forced labor. According to this Katowice Jew, Marion was married and from a good family.

At first, Marion only supplied workers for the Germans, but after a while, he became as much of a Nazi insider as a Jew could be. He would confront the community leaders of Katowice with Nazi demands, and when they were unable to comply, he would use his influence to turn the Germans against the Jews. It was not long before he forced out the community leaders from the *Judenrat* and appointed his own friends in their stead. Finally, he named himself the *Judensalter* of Katowice.

On the orders of the Nazis, Marion extended his activities to other Jewish communities as well. He placed a tax on all the Jews of Sosnowiec, and a larger tax on the wealthiest among them. If they refused or were unable to pay, he had them confined to prison where they were beaten and tortured until they agreed to hand over everything they possessed. A wealthy Jewish iron manufacturer named Furstenberg who refused to pay the tax was stripped naked, tied to a truck, and dragged through the streets of the town until he became unconscious. In his prison cell that night, Furstenberg was visited by Monik Marion. Soon after, he agreed to pay the tax.

One day, Monik Marion, accompanied by a blonde woman whom he introduced as his secretary, arrived in Oswiecim in a Volkswagen driven by a Jew. He was intent upon visiting Leo Shenker in order to learn what had transpired at the meeting in Berlin with Rabbi Leo Baeck. Marion invited Shenker to return to Sosnowiec with him in order to see the work he was doing. On the trip to Sosnowiec, Marion showed Shenker the letter from Himmler, and also admitted that he had an office in the local Gestapo headquarters which took its orders from Eichmann in Berlin.

In Sosnowiec, Marion invited Shenker to dine with him at the elegant community restaurant. During the meal, a messenger came and whispered something in Marion's ear. Marion excused himself and stepped outside the restaurant, where a band of bloodied Jews was marching between a Gestapo company holding aloft flaming torches.

These Jews were the members of the *Judenrat* of Zawiercie, which had been unable to pay the tax of 30,000 marks that Marion had levied. Marion ordered them to pay a portion of the tax immediately, and the remainder at a future date. He then dismissed the Gestapo unit and returned in good spirits to the restaurant.

Shenker left the table and asked to be taken back to Oswiecim. A short time later he received a letter informing him that his services were no longer needed, and that his position as community leader of Oswiecim had been taken over by a Jew named Bernstein from Dabrowa. After spending the following two weeks in prison, Shenker was advised by Marion to take his family and leave Oswiecim. But first he was ordered to collect 30,000 marks f. om the local Jews. Remembering the fate of the Jews of Zawiercie, Shenker collected the money, paid the tax, and prepared to leave Oswiecim with his family.

When Marion was asked by the *Judenrat* of Oswiecim to intercede to save the lives of Baruch Greenbaum and the Waxman brothers who had been sentenced to death, he refused. Shenker, meanwhile, set about leaving Oswiecim armed only with the official documents given to him by the German commander in Oswiecim, a small stash of money hidden deep in his pocket, and the blessing of the Gerer Rebbe. The story of the Rebbe's blessing, as Shenker tells it, is, in itself, wondrous and strange:

I recall a strange and fanstastic story which happened in October, 1939. One morning, I received a telephone call from the *Judenrat* in Krakow. Mr. Biberstein, the head of the Krakow *Judenrat*, told me that the Gerer Rebbe, his family, and close followers were about the pass the Oswiecim train station, and he asked me to bring some warm drinks for them, for in Krakow they would not let Jews approach the Rebbe. They knew that I had special privileges with the Germans for saving their pilot's life when his plane was shot down near my villa.

I called together several leaders of the Oswiecim *kehila*, among them Aharon Silbiger, Avraham Yachtzel, Michael Sandel, Avraham Gross, and Yitzchak Huterer. We took several Thermos bottles of hot tea and some baked goods with us. In the second class train compartment we found the Rebbe sitting entirely isolated, along with his family, some close followers, and his private physician.

The train was guarded by Gestapo agents. I showed them my credentials, and they allowed us to approach the group and give them the food and drinks. The Gerer Rebbe, a short, gray haired man, wearing a wide, tall hat, stood near the window of the compartment to say goodbye to all present. He took my two hands into his and blessed me:

"I pray that you, your wife, and your children will stay alive and go through the war successfully."

The train started to move and we watched it leave the station with the Rebbe. We were then ordered to leave the station area. As we were driving back to town, I noticed sadness on the faces of my co-workers. Some said, "The Rebbe did not wish us well. You he blessed, but not us." I, at the same time, wondered why the Rebbe specifically said, "You, your wife, and your children," and not "your entire family."

Tears came to my eyes and I wondered about the Rebbe's blessing-- was this a curse within a blessing (*kelala b'toch bracha*)? I was thinking about Aryeh, my sister Sala's son, who was, to me, like my own son. He was with me throughout the war, in Bergen-Belsen, and on the night of our liberation he died on the train which carried us out of the camp to freedom.

Aryeh did not have the privilege of seeing the end of the war. My father, a powerful millionaire, died of hunger only one month before the end of the war. In 1942, my sister Liba was handed over by the Polish in Wieliczka to Germans. They took her, together with her two lovely daughters, to the cemetery and shot the two girls and then shot my sister, Liba Hofshteter. My brother Mendel they shot on the way from Wisznice prison to Bochnia. His wife and two children were transferred from Zaloshitz to Belzec. Yitzchak, my sister Sala's second son, was taken with my mother-in-law in a transport to Tarnow. My brother in-law, Zalman Frankel, perished with his wife and children in Krakow. All this happened in 1942. Indeed, a *klala b'toch bracha*.

In spite of everything we went through in ghettos, bunkers, forests, and concentration camp in Bergen-Belsen, we stayed alive, my wife, my children, and I. All this was with the help of *Hashem* and the Gerer Rebbe's blessing.

Chapter 52.
THE END OF JEWISH LIFE IN OSWIECIM

The words, "*Al chayenu ham'surim b'yadecha*"--"For our lives which are in Your hands," spoken several times daily in the "*Modim*" prayer, were deeply ingrained in the hearts of the Jews of Oswiecim. Even as evidence of impending disaster began to mount, most of the merchants of Oswiecim did not sell what they owned and seek to leave town. Rather, so sincere was their faith in God's protection, that when they sold out their goods, they traveled to Lodz to replenish their stock.

But soon enough, the orders came from Berlin to Gestapo agents in Oswiecim to drive the Jews from their shops and to confiscate their belongings. Jews were sent daily to forced labor sites as far away as Germany, and it quickly became apparent that some of these people were not returning home. Death sentences were carried out regularly for arbitrary reasons. The Jews living in Oswiecim before the deportations could see the huge flames rising from the nearby concentration camp.

On April 25, 1941, the Nazis ordered all the Jews of Oswiecim to leave town and travel to Sosnowiec and Bendin. This was the work of Monek Marion, either acting on his own or on orders from above. Thousands of men, women, and children, young and old, carried what remained of their belongings, and walked or traveled in hired wagons along the roads to their fate.

Not only Oswiecim Jews, but Jews from other communities as well, were massed in Sosnowiec, which acquired a very large interim Jewish population. The main leadership consisted of those appointed by the

Nazis, with the *Judenrat,* including some Oswiecim Jews, directly
under them. Some of these Oswiecim Jews in positions of power tried,
at first, to assist their townspeople, but with time it became a bitter
survival struggle and the humanity of a few of these individuals was
compromised. Hoping for rescue from America and England, there
were people who began playing for time and paying money to substitute
other victims when members of their own families had been designated
for deportation. Jews apprehended in the streets were sent to labor
camps in Germany and even in the Sudetenland.

In 1943, the remaining Jews of Oswiecim were about to be deported
to Auschwitz. Many Jewish women, understanding what this boded,
left their children with Polish families. In the best of circumstances,
these were families that the Jewish mothers knew and trusted, but also,
in this grave situation, when there was no alternative, Jewish mothers
surrendered their babies to any stranger who was willing to take them
in. As a result of this situation, many Jewish children were raised as
Catholics. After the war, some surviving parents were able to reclaim
their children from the convents and homes in which they had been
sheltered; others were not. Moreover, there were occasionally children,
such as a young doctor I met in Krakow, who had been lovingly raised
and educated by her Polish parents and could never imagine abandoning
them. On the other hand, a young man I encountered in Sanz at the grave
of Rabbi Chaim Halberstam, who had been raised by a Polish family,
was intensely drawn to his Jewish roots, which ultimately led him to
undergo a *halachic* conversion, circumcision, and accept the chassidic
way of life.

Thus, Oswiecim, once so vital a center of Jewish life and learning,
was entirely emptied of its Jews. Many of the town's Jews perished in
Auschwitz, and only a very small number survived. One such survivor
described to me the madness that overtook the inmates who had
somehow managed to remain at Auschwitz after the Germans evacuated
the camp a short time before the Russians arrived on January 27, 1945.
These inmates pounced on the unguarded food magazines, ripping
through the supplies like ravenous wolves. Then they occupied the
clean and luxurious quarters that the SS abandoned, remaining there
until the official liberation by the Russian army. There were 7,650
inmates left alive in Auschwitz when the Russians liberated the camp,
and the majority of these inmates were Jews.

A woman from Oswiecim whom I met in Miami described to me
how, when Auschwitz was liberated, she decided to walk the two miles

home to search for family and friends. Ulica Berka Yoselowicza, the heart of Oswiecim Jewish life, was, this survivor discovered, entirely destroyed. Hostile strangers now occupied her home and her family's shop in the *Rynek*. She sat down on the steps of a nearby building, hoping some Jews would pass by and invite her into their home. A Pole saw her and asked, "*Tile was zostalo*?" "What, so many of you are still alive?" She heard those words and she fainted. She had survived years of suffering and torture, she had survived Auschwitz, but those words broke her heart.

Chapter 53.
THE ATTEMPT TO REVIVE THE OSWIECIM
COMMUNITY

During the months of March, April, and early May, 1945, following the liberation of Poland by the Russian army, Oswiecim Jews began slowly returning to their town. Chaim Wolnerman, in *Sefer Oshpitzin*, gives an account of his own attempt to go home in those days:

The Red Army freed us from a German concentration camp. The war was still raging. The Allied and Russian Armies were nearing Berlin and the roads were full of soldiers, tanks, cars, and trucks all moving in the direction of Berlin. We were unable in those crucial days to travel by public transportation, and hoped to hitch a ride with some soldiers or civilians. Things were completely disorganized, and we could not trust anyone.

After weeks of wandering, we finally reached "home." We turned to the town's magistrate and police for help in finding Jewish records of the *kehila*. We noticed that there were many young Jews who had also just returned from other camps which had been liberated by the Russians. Some of the young people who fled to Russia during the war followed the Russian army back to Poland until they reached their home towns. Others came out of hiding as soon as the coast was clear.

The response of the magistrates was negative. "We have nothing," they said. The information we received was that all records and lists of Jewish settlers from Oswiecim--records of birth, marriages, death, which were usually kept by the "Metric" Office--were taken by the Germans to Berlin as soon as the Jews were transferred from Oswiecim to the Sosnowiec-Bendin ghetto during April of 1941.

Those returnees had no identification, since they returned almost "naked and barefoot," and for one to stay in town without an I.D. was not permissible. I was instrumental in convincing the authorities, who knew me, to issue I.D.'s to those whom I knew personally. I became a semi-official officer for registering and issuing I.D. cards to Jews.

As soon as the war ended, however, in May of 1945, surviving Jews began returning to Oswiecim at a rapid pace. It was during this period that some of the returnees took the initiative to organize a makeshift Jewish community. Among these survivors was Leo "Eliezer" Shenker, a descendent of one of the most renowned Jewish families in Poland, a family that traced its roots in Oswiecim back to the fifteenth century, and that amassed its fortune in real estate and factories in which thousands of workers were employed. Mr. Shenker gives this account of his coming home:

I returned to Oswiecim together with my wife, children, and my stepmother. We came back as *kaptzonim* (beggars) of the first degree--dehydrated, hungry, wearing torn *shmates* for clothing, and without a *grosh* in our pocket. We stood in the train station of Oswiecim, my city of birth. I hardly recognized it. The train station was enlarged, and dozens of train tracks were added. (This is the area where the concentration camp was located and where trains came bringing inmates from all parts of Poland and neighboring countries.) It was only when we left the station and saw the sign "Hotel Zator" that I realized that we had come to Oswiecim.

Needless to say, we did not recognize any of the people we saw. On the other hand, we saw noisy and drunken Russian soldiers. A kind Polish peasant with a horse and wagon took pity on us when he saw my stepmother falling off her feet. He took us to my villa on Ulica Yagolonska 41. I stood on the steps of the villa--the house from which we fled in the beginning of 1940. A policeman approached and did not let us in, as the police were occupying our villa as their police station. The officer in charge suggested we go to my father's villa, which was situated across the street, and assigned us a room in the attic of the building. The villa was used by the Germans as a hospital for the German civilians who were transferred to Oswiecim from Germany, as well as German military officers.

The following morning, I rose early and went down to bathe in the Sola River. Not a soul could be seen. I could think of the days when the Sola was crowded with Jewish bathers. Even during the early morning hours I could find some Jews who used the Sola as a *mikvah* to immerse themselves before *davening*.

Dr. Moshe Goldberg was always there in the early hours. He was a good friend, leader, and lecturer on behalf of Eretz Yisrael. As I stood there on the shores of the river, I was overwhelmed with a strange feeling which has never left me. I felt as if I returned from another world, after hundreds of years of sleep, to a place familiar to me, but which remained without a soul known to me, without relatives or friends. Only the houses and the panorama remained the same.

As I looked around I had a good view of the city. I was able to see the cement bridge over the Sola, which connected the town from Zasola, the court house, the huge Christian convent, the remnants of what remained of the *mikvah*, including its chimney, but without smoke coming from it. Near there, I observed a bald spot of land where our beloved great synagogue stood, which was destroyed on September 20, 1939, while I was still living in Oswiecim.

I saw the building of the post office on Ulica Yagolonska where Reb Moshe Greenbaum used to live. He built a brick factory near his home, and the area, known as Greenbaum's *Barg* (Greenbaum's hill) was a favorite play ground for the local children.

Returning from the river, I saw the *plantin*, the park, and the remnants of the sports field where I spent many of my young days playing with the other children. When I returned home, my family was still asleep. I thanked the *Ribbono Shel Olam* for giving me the strength, courage, and faith to save the few members of my family. In spite of all the suffering and wandering, we had managed to stay alive. My entire family perished. Only my immediate family survived.

For a few days after their return to Oswiecim, Leo Shenker and his family struggled with sorrow and depression. Then they decided to go to the city hall to register for identification. The officials in charge were complete strangers. As Shenker walked up the steps to the building, he was overcome with horror when he realized that the stones he was treading upon were monuments from the Jewish cemetery that the Nazis had uprooted and used for repairing the sidewalks. This atrocity made him feel that he had to do something to revive at least some element of a Jewish presence to Oswiecim. Yet, at the same time, he was troubled by a nagging question: In the light of all that had happened, was the effort worth while? Even so, Leo Shenker decided to do what he could to restore, at the very least, the town's Jewish cemetery and synagogue.

The entire wall around the cemetery had disappeared. Inside, the graveyard was practically empty. Huge craters pocked the ground where bombs had fallen. All of the marble monuments were gone, some shipped to Germany, and others used to pave roads and patch buildings and stairways. Those monuments that remained had tumbled over and were lying hidden in the tall grass.

In the area where the great synagogue had stood, the surviving Jews discovered a pile of tombstones from the Jewish cemetery. Then, on barges near the Sola River, they found hundreds of marble monuments that had been readied for shipment to Germany. The Jews reclaimed these stones and decided to restore them to their rightful places in the cemetery. Each stone was lovingly placed on top of the correct grave, and Leo Shenker, Heshek Kinreich, and others worked tirelessly to erect a new fence around the entire cemetery.

One survivor decided to open a grocery store on the outskirts of town. When he was advised by his fellow Jews to be cautious, he declared that he was not afraid and that many of the local citizens were his friends. One night, Polish thieves entered his home and murdered him. This was the first Jew to be buried in the the restored cemetery.

The returning Jews of Oswiecim also needed a synagogue in which to pray. Most of the houses of worship had been destroyed, but the Chevra Mishnayot Synagogue on Ulica Kosczelna, not far from Ulica Yoselowicza, was still standing, though it had been seriously damaged. Before the war, this synagogue, generously endowed by the wealthy Jews of the town, had stood on the street along with two others, facing the back of the police station. Indeed, the joke in town used to be that a religious Jew incarcerated in the police station could open the window of his cell and pray with the *minyan* at the Chevra Mishnayot. The Synagogue, distinguished by its beautiful women's section, had been extremely active in its time, with *minyanim* from early morning to noon. On Shabbat and holidays, it was filled to capacity. Rabbi Yankele Pomarner, the son-in-law of the Sassover Rebbe, officiated there until a few years before the outbreak of the war, when he went on to become the *Admor* of Sassov in Komarno. The leaders of the Chevra Mishnayot Synagogue, including Reb Yakir Singer, Reb Alter Nerberg, and Reb Avraham Ringer, then appointed the *Dayan*, Rabbi Chaim Yudel Halberstam, as their spiritual leader. They also engaged as its *chazzan* the popular Reb Avraham Yehoshua Wilchford, and, in addition to all this, they were privileged to have the famous *Maggid*, Reb Mordechai Boruch Donner, deliver his *mussar drashot* every Sabbath afternoon.

It was the Chevra Mishnayot Synagogue that the Jewish returnees to Oswiecim decided to refurbish as their facility. They found it very difficult to form a daily *minyan*, but on Sabbath and holidays they were successful in holding services, although their efforts were often greeted by a barrage of rocks thrown through the synagogue windows by the local anti-Semites. At the same time, news reached the Oswiecim survivors of attempts to pull Jews off trains in order to murder them, of the killing of Jews fleeing over the mountains to Czechoslovakia, and of the pogrom in Kielce. Oswiecim Jews, in those days, were also often approached by Poles who offered to sell them Jewish children who had been harbored during the war. Also offered for sale were Torah scrolls and Jewish artifacts that the Poles had expropriated.

For close to ten years, attempts were made to reestablish Jewish life in Oswiecim, but without success. The local Poles made the lives of the Jews miserable. Indeed, with the shadow of the millions of dead at Auschwitz looming so close at hand, Oswiecim could no longer be a place for living Jews. Jews left for Israel, America, and others countries. On my first return visit to Oswiecim, there were only two Jewish couples in the town, the Kupermans and the Zeidbands. Today, there is one lone Jew.

A short time after the fence was installed around the cemetery, it was destroyed by Polish youths, along with many of the monuments. At one point, town officials declared their intention to raze the cemetery and to sell the land in parcels to build homes and apartment houses. Only vigorous protest from many places dissuaded them from carrying out this plan.

Today, the Jewish cemetery in Oswiecim is one of the few in Poland still standing in good order, thanks to the benefactions of the Sharf family. The walls are intact and the iron gate is locked with a caretaker in charge. The monuments are upright, although many do not stand in their correct places. A visitor can stop by and say a prayer. But not far from the town itself, on its outskirts, is perhaps the largest Jewish cemetery in the world--Auschwitz. At Auschwitz there are not, and there never have been, stones or monuments or individual graves for the dead. The bones and ashes of the dead cover the ground at Auschwitz, and even if a fence could be built around this horrific cemetery, there will never be any way to encompass its horrors in the imagination.

Chapter 54.
AUSCHWITZ

How can a Jewish visitor to Krakow and Katowice, especially one who had spent his youth in the town of Oswiecim or Oshpitzin, stay away from Auschwitz? Less than an hour's drive from Krakow, two miles from Oswiecim, Auschwitz, in the words of one of the witnesses at the Eichmann trial, was another planet: "Auschwitz was a planet....The time there was not a concept as we perceive it here on our planet. Every fraction of a second that passed there was at a different rate of time. And the inhabitants of that planet had no names, no parents, and no children. They were not clothed as we are clothed here. They were not born there and they did not conceive there. They breathed and lived according to different laws of nature. They did not live according to this world of ours and they did not die."

It was a pleasant, sunny morning when I set out for Auschwitz, stopping first for prayers at the Remu Synagogue in Krakow. After prayers, I stepped into the courtyard to bid farewell to the ten regulars gathered there, shaking hands with each one, and leaving some of the contents of my hand in theirs. "Last year you gave us more," one of them complained. I reached for my wallet and repeated the handshake. This time, the beggar was satisfied.

In the courtyard I met two reporters for *The Jerusalem Post*, Kaleb Ben David and Naomi Schrier, whom I had met earlier in the Warsaw synagogue. They had come to cover the Jewish Festival that would be held the next day in Krakow. I invited them to join me in the cab to Auschwitz.

On the way to the camp we passed Chrzanow, Trzebinia, and many other familiar towns. Recalling a comment by Czeslaw Jakubowicz, the president of the Krakow Jewish community, to the effect that the Festival stirred up anti-Semitism and that the Jews would be better off without it, I raised the subject with my traveling companions. Kaleb Ben David voiced the opinion that Polish youth were interested in Jewish culture and that the Festival was a sign that the Poles wanted to be forgiven for the acts they had committed. A discussion then ensued about the nature of the Polish attitude toward Jews, and whether the entrenched anti-Semitism could really be uprooted. I recalled for the two young reporters an observation made to me by eighteen-year-old Voitek in Lublin: "You cannot educate the Polish people to love the Jews, no matter what you do for them."

The Auschwitz concentration camp was bustling with visitors. Teachers were leading groups of students through the various blocks; some seemed sad, others were smiling. Only very seldom could the word "Jews" be heard in any of the explanations by the guides. For the uninformed visitor to Auschwitz, what happened in this horrific place happened to Polish citizens as a consequence of Nazi aggression. In Block 27, however, there is a new display with a sign at the entrance: "*Historica Martyrologia Zhydow.*" Here, Jewish artifacts and photographs are on display, but this section of the camp is visited by few people who are not Jewish.

Nearly half a century ago, the Russians liberated the Auschwitz camp and the Polish government decided that it would be maintained and preserved just as it had been found. Indeed, the site has become a popular tourist attraction. The visitor views, in silence, the workings of the camp, the torture rooms, and the cell blocks. Block 11, known as "*Block Smierci*" (Death Block) is especially popular. This is where the Nazis shot at close range those inmates who failed to obey orders.

On display at the Auschwitz camp are mountains of valises bearing identifying tags with mostly Jewish names. Exhibits include mounds of children's shoes, hair brushes, eyeglasses, Jewish religious articles, and human hair. The Nazis confiscated over fifty million dollars in currency from their Jewish victims, not including vast amounts of gold, silver, and diamonds.

For Jews and all people of good will, these displays are truly heart-rending. But there is no doubt that for some of the visitors, Auschwitz is little more than another museum at best, and, at worst, for the anti-Semites among those visitors, it represents the fulfillment of their most vile imaginings. It is well known that sordid anti-Semitic jokes still abound. *Harper's* Magazine once listed some of them. How many Jews can be fit into a Volkswagen? Answer: 506; six in the seats and 500 in the ashtrays. A mother admonishes a child who is fiddling with a bar of soap, "Stop playing with Anne Frank." Two Jewish children are sitting on a rooftop, near a chimney. "What are you doing up there?" a passerby asks. "We're waiting for our parents," they reply. A Jew walks down the street carrying a canister of gas connected by a pipe to his mouth. "'I'm addicted," he explains to anyone who inquires. Why did so many Jews go to Auschwitz? Answer: The fare was free. There are many more such jokes, and what they testify to is a kind of grim fascination with and relishing of the fate of the Jews, and a persistence, even in the face of such unspeakable atrocities, of age-old anti-Semitic stereotypes.

The Carmelite convent at Auschwitz that has recently been the subject of so much controversy is also a manifestation of ancient anti-Semitic canards. The nuns claim to be praying for the salvation of the souls of the Jews slaughtered in the camp there. Indeed, the very presence of a Catholic institution at this site, which according to a United Nations agreement is required to be left intact, represents an attempt by the Church to identify itself with the Holocaust and thereby nullify its unforgivable indifference to the plight of the Jews in the days that they were being transported and exterminated in masses. And although the Church has agreed to move the convent, a visitor observes nuns moving serenely about, tending the garden and genuflecting in front of the twenty-four-foot cross erected there, which seems to be freshly painted. Moreover, an addition is being built to the existing structure, and the piles of bricks, sand, and gravel that are in evidence everywhere all belie the Church's claim that the nuns will soon be moving.

Upon leaving the death camp at Auschwitz/Birkenau, I stopped in the town to visit Shimek Kluger, the last remaining Jew in Oswiecim. He offered me refreshments and an hour of gentle conversation, in which he reiterated his hope to leave Poland soon and join his brother and his family in Brooklyn, New York. Before departing, I presented him with a *talit*, a *mezuzah*, and two yarmulkes.

From Mr. Kluger's house, I went to visit the *Rynek* and Berka Yoselowicza Street, where the great synagogue once stood. I stopped at the dilapidated old house where my first *melamed*, Reb Lazar, taught me the *alef-bet*. I then visited the apartment in which I spent my youth, on

Ulica Parkowa, near the park. The Poles who occupy the apartment at present were kind enough to let me look around, and I inquired of them if the landlord of the house, Mr. Soltys, still lived there.

I was led to Mr. Soltys' residence, where I found him lying in bed. He was one hundred years old. Mr. Soltys took one look at me and said, "*Ty yescse zyjesz?*" "You're still alive?" Much to his dismay, I assured him that except for Poland and a few other countries, Jews are thriving, particularly in the United States and in Israel. Upon hearing this news, Soltys' face grew red with rage, and I left him without saying good-bye.

Chapter 55.
POLAND REVISITED

Mornings and evenings in Warsaw, as I accompanied Rabbi Joskowicz, Poland's Chief Rabbi, to synagogue, young and middle-aged passersby stared openly at my bearded companion dressed in his long black gabardine and wide-brimmed chassidic hat. Some opened their mouths and called out *"Zhyd"* or other unflattering words. In Poland today there is simply no other Jew who looks like Rabbi Joskowicz. I expressed my concern for his safety. It would require only one idealistic anti-Semite to do him injury, I pointed out, and unfortunately, there are many in the cities and towns of Poland. As a result of the open displays of bigotry that I encountered during my walks with the Rabbi, I suggested to the leaders of the Warsaw community that a *shamash* be appointed to accompany him wherever he goes, for in such a hostile atmosphere, even a simple trip to the market is not without its dangers.

Even with only a pitiful remnant of Jewish life in Poland, the visitor cannot help but be struck by the pervasiveness of anti-Semitic incidents and by the persistence of this irrational hatred despite the tragic historical realities. On April 29, 1990, for example, during one of my visits, there was an anti-Semitic attack in Kielce on a Jewish Klezmer group from Vinnetza in the Ukraine that was performing at the international Jewish folk festival in Krakow. The details about this incident were supplied to me by Dr. Shimon Samuels, the European director of the Simon Wiesenthal Center, whom I accompanied on a day-long visit to Lublin, Sobibor, and Maidanek. According to Dr.

Samuels, the anti-Semites smashed the car belonging to the Klezmer group and then threw a gas grenade into the theater, injuring several members of the audience. The authorities, claiming that this was an attack directed against the Soviets rather than the Jews, took no action and made no arrests.

The persistence of anti-Semitism in Kielce is particularly disturbing because this, of course, is the city where a savage pogrom took place immediately after the war. Before the Second World War, 25,000 Jews lived in Kielce. Afterward, 200 returned from the extermination and labor camps. On July 4, 1946, 42 of these survivors were murdered in cold blood by local Poles.

Dr. Samuels went on to describe to me a Polish nationalist conference he had attended in Warsaw on the first of May along with 3,000 of the city's residents. Openly anti-Semitic literature was distributed at this gathering, and the atmosphere was poisoned with venomous and crude anti-Jewish remarks by speaker after speaker and by members of the audience. Even so, Dr. Samuels expressed the hope that, through cultural links and other cooperative projects, the Polish citizenry could be re-educated and enlightened, and he took pains to praise Henryk Woznakowsky, the spokesman for the Krakow Jewish Festival, for his efforts in promoting better understanding between Poles and Jews. Mr. Jakubowicz, on the other hand, the head of the Krakow Jewish community, was of the opinion that the festival would have a harmful effect, arousing latent anti-Semitism, and that while it might inspire outside Jews who come to the city for the event itself, it would do little good for the existing Krakow Jewish community. For his part, Mr. Jakubowicz much preferred efforts, such as the kind I and others had been organizing over the years, of collecting religious articles and other goods, and distributing them in every town and village in Poland where even only one aged Jew remained.

Dr. Shimon Samuels' optimism notwithstanding, again and again the visitor is confronted with evidence attesting to the entrenchment of anti-Semitic attitudes in Poland. On the road to Lublin, for example, we passed a huge billboard upon which the word "*Zhyd*" had been smeared, accompanied by Stars of David and an obscenity that my taxi driver was too embarrassed to translate. The driver had to conclude that this could not have been the work of children, for the sign, fifteen feet from the ground, required a ladder to reach, and a great deal of relatively sophisticated malicious planning and organization was necessary to execute this anti-Semitic graffiti.

In Lublin itself I encountered a young man who could, in many ways, be described as a casualty of Polish anti-Semitism. I visited the city on a Sunday, in the company of Dr. Shimon Samuels, and went directly to the little Jewish museum. This museum, the pet project of Dr. Simcha Vais, who was born in Lublin, and was, until recently, the leader of the Warsaw Jewish community, is open on Sundays and Thursdays from ll A.M. to 1 P.M. It is housed in a small synagogue on Ulica Lubartowska 10 on the first floor; there are some shops on the ground floor, and Polish families occupy the apartments on the floors above it. As I was about to enter the museum at about ten o'clock in the morning, I was approached by a handsome young man, about eighteen years old, who asked me in broken English what I was looking for. "*Boznica Zhydowska*," I replied, "the Jewish synagogue." He said that this was also where he was going, and together we waited for the caretaker to open the museum.

There was something unusual about this young man. While most Poles were in church on Sunday morning, he was visiting a synagogue. He opened his briefcase and offered me some orange juice. Did he want money? I wondered. But when I offered him some, he handed it back to me. And although his features suggested that he might be Jewish, when I inquired, he declared he was not. Yet when I gently probed a bit deeper, he did admit that he had a Jewish grandmother who had married a Christian. Her son, this young man's uncle, although married to a Christian himself, is nevertheless called "*Zhyd*" by the townspeople. The young man's mother, also married to a Catholic, is a dentist and would like her son to become a doctor. The young man, for his part, had often accompanied his father to church but felt troubled and unhappy there, and so this morning he had come to the little Jewish museum in the synagogue.

I invited him to accompany me on a visit to the Lublin cemetery. When we arrived there, the caretaker informed us that the new monument being erected was financed by a wealthy Belgian Jew who had been born in Lublin, and that the building would eventually house a Jewish museum. I recited a *Molei* at one of the monuments, and noticed, as I did so, that my young companion covered his head with his hand and whispered "Amen" when I concluded the prayer.

When we returned to the synagogue museum I was informed that the *parasolnik* (umbrella man), Nahum Schicz, the last Jew in Lublin, had passed away. I visited his widow who thanked me profusely for the packages of clothing I had been sending to her family over the years. She informed me that her daughter was now an actress in the Warsaw Yiddish theater, and, indeed, I had an opportunity to meet this young woman several days later in the Warsaw synagogue. While in Lublin, I also revisited the Yeshiva Chachmei Lublin building which is now occupied by a medical school.

As we made plans to leave Lublin and go on to Maidanek, the young man asked if he might accompany us. "It is the only place where I can cry," he said. When we were about to leave the camp, I once again offered him money, and again he refused. He opened his briefcase as he had done earlier, but this time, instead of orange juice, he took out a pistol--an Italian Baretta. Be prepared to say *Shema*, I thought to myself. But noticing my alarm, the young man was quick to reassure me. He always carried a weapon, he explained, because he was in constant danger of being attacked by anti-Semites. "You cannot educate the Polish people to love Jews, no matter what you do for them," he declared.

These words, spoken from the front lines, as it were, were uttered by the young man in the presence of Dr. Shimon Samuels. They may well have inspired some second thoughts in the mind of the European director of the Simon Wiesenthal Center about the feasibility of "tackling the problems of anti-Semites frontally by developing educational projects in cooperation with the Polish government."

At midnight, a day after the Klezmer group was assaulted in Kielce, the Jewish cemetery in Lublin was vandalized and eleven monuments of the 54 restored in 1987 were desecrated, some removed entirely and others smashed against the ground and destroyed. Among these monuments was that of the Maharshal, Rabbi Shlomo Luria, who died in 1873 and was the author of many *Gaonic* volumes. He was the first rabbi to receive the title of Rector of the Yeshiva of Lublin from the Polish king. The stone of Rabbi Meir ben Gedalya, the Maharam of Lublin (died 1616), was also vandalized. The Maharam was a great Talmudic and *Halachic* authority who served as *Dayan* and *Rosh Yeshiva* in Krakow, Lvov, and finally in Lublin. Fortunately, the oldest monuments of the cemetery--those of Yitzchak Halevi Kopelman (1541), Reb Shalom Shachna (1558), and Rabbi Yaakov Yitzchak Hurwic, the Chozeh of Lublin, whose grave is visited annually by hundreds of petitioners who leave *kvitlach*, light candles, and recite prayers--were spared.

What is it about Jewish graves that invites such savagery? Even a dead Jew is not allowed to rest in peace. Recently, on a visit to the

Bobover Rebbe's grave, I noticed some filthy expressions painted on one side of the enclosure. When I asked the twelve-year-old son of my taxi driver to read what was written, he blushed deeply and declared he could not. "Why would anyone want to write such things on the tomb of a dead person?" the boy asked. "What good would it do him?"

In the light of this unrelenting, ongoing anti-Semitism, then, and in the light of the unspeakable atrocities of the past, why do some Jews continue to remain in Poland? The answers, of course, are varied and complex--as varied and complex as the individuals involved--but a few general themes do emerge. Of the pitiful few who remain in Poland, the majority regard themselves as too old to make so drastic a change as to emigrate and abandon everything they know. Many are married to non-Jews who, they feel, would be uncomfortable in Israel or the United States and would be regarded as outcasts. And some fear that a move would be too financially risky. So they stay where they are, enduring painful memories and continual hostility for the sake of a meager pension and an allotment of forty dollars several times a year from the Joint Distribution Committee.

The persistent anti-Semitism in Poland also obliges the Jewish visitor to re-examine his or her motives for traveling to this troubled land and contributing to its economy as a tourist. Why bother going back there at all? Why not put Poland and all that it represents behind us?

For my part, I go to Poland for my own sake and for the sake of my fellow Jews. For my own sake, I go because I have never quite given up the hope of finding some relative who may have survived; I go to visit the remaining cemeteries, to recite a prayer at the graves of my family, of rabbis and *tzaddikim*; I go to see with my own eyes the extermination camps and the monuments, the synagogues, the museums, and the memorials that attest to the world of my childhood and youth, the world of Oswiecim, once so bright and joyful, that became the black, tortured hell of Auschwitz.

And I go to Poland in order to do what I can for the sake of my fellow Jews--those inside that cursed land and those outside. For those inside, I can bring gifts of religious articles, worldly goods to ease their poverty, and the simple comfort that comes through human contact and the knowledge that they are not alone, that Jews in other countries care about them. And for the sake of those Jews outside Poland, I can make my way to every little town and village and hamlet on the Polish landscape, seek out the last Jew, find what remains there of Jewish life.

And having done so, I can come out of this heart to darkness to give my testimony. I can bear witness.

From my repeated visits to Poland, the single truth that has been reinforced for me is the sheer preciousness of the State of Israel. If there is one lesson for our people from Polish-Jewish history, that lesson is that Israel is absolutely necessary. Poland, which for centuries had been a home for Jews, has become a graveyard. Israel will always be home.

At an Independence Day celebration in the Warsaw villa of the Israeli ambassador to Poland, I toasted the existence of the State of Israel with a large crowd that included Pinchas Menachem Joskowicz, Poland's Chief Rabbi, representatives of the Jewish communities and cultural societies, editors of the Yiddish newspaper, the *Folkshtimme*, a Catholic cardinal and bishop, and the United States Ambassador to Poland, John Davis. When Mr. Davis observed that despite the crowd in the room, people were able to move about freely, I explained to him that inside the ambassador's home, we were, after all, standing on Israeli territory. In ancient times in Israel, I went on to elaborate, on festival days in the Holy Temple, people would be packed in the courtyard, yet when it came time to prostrate themselves and kneel and bow in prayer, there was always ample room.

In Israel, too, there is, and there always will be, room. For the Jews of Africa and Asia, for the Jews of North and South America, for the Jews of Ethiopia and Russia, for the Jews of Europe whose childhood Oswiecims have been twisted and distorted and perverted into Auschwitzes, there is, and there always will be, one place on this earth where there will always be room. In Israel there will always be room.

AFTERWORD

Auschwitz, 1959

There I stood on a little hill
in the Auschwitz Death Camp
surrounded by blocks and barracks
where inmates lived, suffered, died
under the black smokestacks of the ovens,
encircled by the stark whiteness of snow and ash and bone.
The Polish guide explained,
"The grass on these plains
grows abundantly in summer and spring,
blue grass fed by the fertilizer under the soil.
Come back after winter and see how lovely it is!"

There I stood, praying the ashes could somehow cohere,
Recalling the question posed to Ezekiel in the valley,
"Can these bones live?"
And there came a noise, a shaking, and the bones
came together, bone to his bone,
the sinews and the flesh upon them,
and the skin covered them above,
and the breath came into them and they lived,
and stood up upon their feet, an exceeding great army.
"Behold O my people,
I will open your graves,
And cause you to come out of your graves,
And bring you to the land of Israel."

There I stood, on a lofty mountain
in Jerusalem.
Before me, the vast host of the Jewish people,
In schoolrooms, in cities, in factories, in villages,
In battle, in peace.
God, remember the souls of the departed
and guard over the resurrected children of Israel
in the land of Israel

Jerusalem, 1993